MW01231949

WOOD PELLET SMOKER & GRILL COOKBOOK

2 BOOKS IN 1:

100 QUICK AND EFFORTLESS RECIPES TO MAKE YOUR BARBECUES THE ENVY OF YOUR NEIGHBORHOOD

JORDAN WOOD

Table of Contents

Table of Contents: Wood Pellet Smoker Cookbook

WOOD PELLET GRILL COOKBOOK

50 EASY AND MOUTHWATERING BBQ RECIPES TO ENJOY AND COOK FOR YOUR FAMILY AND FRIENDS

JORDAN WOOD

Introduction

A pellet grill is essentially a multi-functional grill which has been so designed that the compressed wood pellets end up being the real source of fuel. They are outdoor cookers and tend to combine the different striking elements of smokers, gas grills, ovens, and even charcoal. The very reason which has cemented their popularity since ages have to be the kind of quality and flavor that they tend to infuse in the food you make on them.

Not only this, by varying the kind of wood pellet you are using, but you can also bring in the variation in the actual flavor of the food as well. Often, the best chefs use a mix and match technique of wood pellets to infuse the food with their signature flavor that have people hooked to their cooking in no time.

The clinical definition of a wood pellet smoker grill is smoking, grilling, roasting, and baking barbecue using compressed hardwood sawdust such as apple, cherry, hickory, maple, mesquite, oak, and other wood pellets. It is a pit. Wood pellet smoker grills provide the flavor profile and moisture that only hardwood dishes can achieve. Depending on the manufacturer and model, the grill temperature on many models can be well over 150 ° F to 600 ° F. Gone are the days when people say they cannot bake on wood pellet smoking grills!

Wood pellet smoker grills offer the succulence, convenience, and safety not found in charcoal or gas grills. The smoke here is not as thick as other smokers common to you. Its design provides the versatility and benefits of a convection oven. *A wood pellet smoker grill is safe and easy to operate.*

How do they work?

The grill would run on electricity and therefore it needs to be plugged in for the sake of deriving power. The design is such that pellets have to be added to the hopper that in turn will funnel down owing to the presence of a rotating auger and a motor.

The auger aims to make sure that the pellets get pushed down to the fire pot at the pre-configured speed which is determined by the yard control panel showing the temperature. As soon as the pellets reach the fire pot, there is an ignition rod that creates a flame that in turn causes the production of smoke.

Also, a fan is present at the bottom which helps in pushing both the generated heat and smoke upwards on the grill and thereby allows for the convection style of even cooking.

This happens to be the basic mechanism of the working of a wood pellet grill. Knowing the different parts of the wood pellet grill and also the working mechanism will prepare you in a much better way to ensure that you can use the grill in the right manner.

However, before we venture further into the recipes, we are going to shift our focus on some important points about these grills. This is because the right knowledge is crucial to ensuring that you know what you are getting into.

Beef

Smoked Rib-Eye Steaks

Preparation Time: 5 minutes

Cooking Time: 50 minutes

Servings: 2

Ingredients:

- 2 thick rib-eye steaks (1.5-lbs, 0.68-kgs)
- Salt and black pepper
- Steak rubs, of choice

Directions:

Allow the steaks to sit out at room Smoke Temperature for half an hour.

Season the steaks with salt, black pepper, and your choice of rub. Arrange the steaks directly on the grill and cook for just over 20 minutes.

Take the streaks off the grill and set the Smoke Temperature to 400°F (205°C).

Sear the cooked steaks on the hotter grill for 5 minutes on each side.

Wrap the steaks in kitchen foil and set aside for 10 minutes to rest.

Slice and serve with your choice of sides.

Nutrition:

Calories: 615

Total Fat: 43g

Saturated Fat: 19g

Cholesterol: 177mg

Sodium: 205mg

Texan-Style Smoke Beef Brisket

Preparation Time: 30 minutes

Cooking Time: 15 hours

Servings: 18

Ingredients:

- 1 whole packet brisket, refrigerated (14-lb, 6.3-kgs)
- Sea salt – 2 tablespoons
- Garlic powder – 2 tablespoons
- Coarsely ground black pepper – 2 tablespoons

Directions:

Remove the brisket from the fridge and flip over so that the point end is directly on the worktop. Remove and discard any excess fat or silver skin from the muscle. Carefully, trim the fat section until smooth between the point end and the flat end. Trim and discard loose fat or meat from the point. Square both the edges and the end of the flat. Finally, flip the meat over and trim the top to an approximate thickens ½-ins (1.25-cms) across the surface of the meat.

In a bowl, combine the rub ingredients, sea salt, garlic powder and black pepper. Rub the seasoning all over the brisket.

Arrange the meat on the smoker with the pointed end facing towards the main heat source. Close the smoker lid and smoke for approximately 8 hours, or until a meat thermometer registers 165°F (74°C).

On a large, clean work surface roll out a large piece of aluminum foil and place your brisket in the middle. Wrap the meat, by folding the foil edge over edge to create a leaf-proof seal all the way around. Return the foil-wrapped brisket to the smoker, seam side facing downwards.

Close the smoker's lid and continue to cook at 225°F (110°C). A meat thermometer inserted in the thickest part of the brisket needs to register 202°F (108°C). This will take between 5-8 hours.

When cooked, transfer the meat to a chopping board and set to one side to rest for 60 minutes before slicing.

When you are ready to serve, slice the point and flat against the grain. Serve.

Nutrition:

Calories: 282kcal

Carbohydrates: 1g

Protein: 36g

Fat: 1g

Saturated Fat: 4g

Sodium: 775mg

Potassium: 19mg

Vitamin A: 5IU

Calcium: 4mg

Iron: 0.1mg

Delicious Soy Marinated Steak

Preparation Time: 20 minutes

Cooking Time: 55 minutes

Servings: 4

Ingredients:

- 1/2 chopped onion
- .3 chopped cloves of garlic
- 1/4 cup of olive oil
- 1/4 cup of balsamic vinegar
- 1/4 cup of soy sauce
- 1 tablespoon of Dijon mustard

- 1 tablespoon of rosemary
- 1 teaspoon of salt to taste
- 1/2 teaspoon of ground black pepper to taste
- 1 1/2 pounds of flank steak

Directions:

Using a large mixing bowl, add in all the ingredients on the list aside from the steak then mix properly to combine.

Place the steak in a Ziploc bag, pour in the prepared marinade then shake properly to coat.

Place the bag in the refrigerator and let the steak marinate for about thirty minutes to two full days.

Preheat the Wood Pellet Smoker and Grill to 350-400 degrees F, remove the steak from its marinade then set the marinade aside for blasting.

Place the steak on the preheated grill then grill for about six to eight minutes until the beef is heated through.

Flip the steak over and cook for an additional six minutes until an inserted thermometer reads 150 degrees F.

Place the steak on a cutting board and let rest for about five minutes. Slice and serve.

Nutrition:

Calories: 300

Fat: 20g

Carbs: 8g

Protein: 22g

Smoked Italian Meatballs

Preparation Time: 10 minutes

Cooking Time: 30 minutes

Servings: 8

Ingredients:

- 1-pound ground beef
- 1-pound Italian Sausage
- ½ cup Italian breadcrumbs
- 1 teaspoon dry mustard
- ½ cup parmesan cheese (grated)
- 1 teaspoon Italian seasoning
- 1 jalapeno (finely chopped)

- 2 eggs
- 1 teaspoon salt
- 1 onion (finely chopped)
- 2 teaspoon garlic powder
- ½ teaspoon smoked paprika
- 1 teaspoon oregano
- 1 teaspoon crushed red pepper
- 1 tablespoon Worcestershire sauce

Directions:

Combine all the ingredients in a large mixing bowl. Mix until the ingredients are well combined.

Mold the mixture into 1 ½ inch balls and arrange the balls into a greased baking sheet.

Preheat the wood pellet smoker to 180°F, using hickory pellet.

Arrange the meatballs on the grill and smoke for 20 minutes.

Increase the griller's temperature to 350°F and smoke until the internal temperature of the meatballs reaches 165°F.

Remove the meatballs from the grill and let them cool for a few minutes.

Serve warm and enjoy.

Nutrition:

Carbohydrates: 12 g

Protein: 28 g

Fat: 16 g

Sodium: 23 mg

Cholesterol: 21 mg

Braised Short Ribs

Preparation Time: 25 minutes

Cooking Time: 4 hours

Servings: 2 to 4

Ingredients:

4 beef short ribs

Salt

Freshly ground black pepper

½ cup beef broth

Directions:

Supply your smoker with wood pellets and follow the manufacturer's specific start-up procedure. With the lid closed, let the grill heat to 180°F.

Season the ribs on both sides with salt and pepper.

Place the ribs directly on the grill grate and smoke for 3 hours.

Pull the ribs from the grill and place them on enough aluminum foil to wrap them completely.

Increase the grill's temperature to 375°F.

Fold in three sides of the foil around the ribs and add the beef broth. Fold in the last side, completely enclosing the ribs and liquid.

Return the wrapped ribs to the grill and cook for 45 minutes more.

Remove the short ribs from the grill, unwrap them, and serve immediately.

Master Tip

Adding herbs to your wrap, such as rosemary or thyme, can contribute some fresh, delicious flavor to the short ribs.

Nutrition:

Calories: 240

Fat: 23g

Carbohydrates: 1g

Dietary Fiber 0g

Protein: 33g

Grilled Steak and Vegetable Kebabs

Preparation Time: 15 minutes

Cooking Time: 20 minutes

Servings: 5

Ingredients:

Marinade

1/4 cup of olive oil

1/4 cup of soy sauce

1 1/2 tablespoons of fresh lemon juice

1 1/2 tablespoons of red wine vinegar

2 1/2 tablespoons of Worcestershire sauce

1 tablespoon of honey

2 teaspoons of Dijon mustard

1 tablespoon of garlic

1 teaspoon of freshly ground black pepper to taste

Kebabs

1 3/4 lbs. of sirloin steak

1 sliced zucchini.

3 sliced bell peppers

1 large and sliced red onion

1 tablespoon of olive oil

Salt and freshly ground black pepper to taste

1/2 teaspoon of garlic powder

Directions:

Using a large mixing bowl, add in the oil, soy sauce, lemon juice, red wine vinegar, Worcestershire sauce, Dijon, honey, garlic, and pepper to taste then mix properly to combine.

Using a sharp knife, cut the steak into smaller pieces or cubes then add to a resealable bag.

Pour the marinade into the bag with steak then shake to coat. Let the steak marinate for about three to six hours in the refrigerator.

Preheat the Wood Pellet Smoker and Grill to 425 degrees F, place the veggies into a mixing bowl, add in oil, garlic powder, salt, and pepper to taste then mix to combine.

Thread the veggies and steak alternately unto skewers, place the skewers on the preheated grill and grill for about eight to nine minutes until it is cooked through.

Make sure you turn the kebabs occasionally as you cook. Serve.

Nutrition:

Calories: 350; Fat: 14g; Carbs: 18g; Protein: 34g

Grilled Barbecue Beef Ribs

Preparation Time: 30 minutes

Cooking Time: 1 hour

Servings: 4

Ingredients:

- 1/2 cup of Dijon mustard
- 2 tablespoons of cider vinegar
- 3 lbs. of spareribs
- 4 tablespoons of paprika powder
- 1/2 tablespoon of chili powder
- 1 1/2 tablespoon of garlic powder

- 2 teaspoons of ground cumin
- 2 teaspoon of onion powder
- 1 1/2 tablespoon of ground black pepper to taste
- 2 tablespoons of salt to taste
- 2 tablespoons of butter which is optional

Directions:

Preheat a Wood Pellet Smoker and Grill to 350 degrees F, using a small mixing bowl, add in the mustard and the vinegar then mix properly to combine.

Rub the mixture on the spareribs, coating all sides. Using another mixing bowl, add in the paprika powder, chili powder, garlic powder, cumin, onion powder, salt, and pepper to taste then mix properly to combine.

Reserve a small quantity of the mixture, seasoned the spareribs with the rest of the spice mixture, coating all sides.

Wrap the seasoned ribs in aluminum foil, top with the butter if desired then place the ribs on the preheated grill.

Grill the ribs for about one hour until it is cooked through. Make sure you flip after every twenty minutes.

Once the ribs are cooked through, remove from the grill, unwrap the aluminum foil then grill the ribs for another two to five minutes until crispy.

Let the ribs cool for a few minutes, slice, and serve.

Nutrition:

Calories: 280

Fat: 42g

Cholesterol: 94mg

Carbs: 6g

Protein: 55g

Pork

Smoked Pork Loin

Preparation Time: 15 minutes

Cooking Time: 3 hours

Servings: 4

Ingredients:

- ½ quart apple juice
- ½ quart apple cider vinegar
- ½ cup of sugar

- ¼ cup of salt
- 2 tablespoons fresh ground pepper
- 1 pork loin roast
- ½ cup Greek seasoning

Directions:

Take a large container and make the brine mix by adding apple juice, vinegar, salt, pepper, sugar, liquid smoke, and stir

Keep stirring until the sugar and salt have dissolved and added the loin

Add more water if needed to submerge the meat

Cover and chill overnight

Pre-heat your smoker to 250 degrees Fahrenheit with hickory Preferred Wood Pellet

Coat the meat with Greek seasoning and transfer to your smoker

Smoker for 3 hours until the internal Smoke Temperature of the thickest part registers 160 degrees Fahrenheit

Serve and enjoy!

Nutrition:

Calories: 169

Fats: 5g

Carbs: 3g

Fiber: 3g

Strawberry and Jalapeno Smoked Ribs

Preparation Time: 15 minutes

Cooking Time: 3 hours

Servings: 4

Ingredients:

- 3 tablespoons salt
- 2 tablespoons ground cumin
- 1 tablespoon dried oregano

- 1 tablespoon garlic, minced
- 2 teaspoons chili powder
- 1 teaspoon ground black pepper
- 1 teaspoon celery seed
- 1 teaspoon dried thyme
- 1 rack spareribs
- 2 slabs baby back pork ribs
- 1 cup apple juice
- 2 jalapeno peppers, cut half in lengthwise, deseeded
- ½ cup beer
- ½ cup onion, chopped
- ¼ cup sugar-free strawberry
- 3 tablespoons BBQ sauce
- 1 tablespoon olive oil
- 2 garlic cloves
- Salt and pepper to taste

Directions:

Take a bowl and add salt, oregano, cumin, and minced garlic, 1 teaspoon of ground black pepper, chili powder, ground thyme, and celery seed

Transfer the mix to a food processor

Place your baby back rib slabs and spare rib rack on sheets of aluminum foil and rub the spice mix all over their body

Fold up the foil around each of them

Divide and pour the apple juice amongst the foil packets and foil the edges together to seal them up

Let them marinate for about 8 hours or overnight

Prepare your oven rack and place it about 6 inches away from Preferred Wood Pellet source and pre-heat your oven's broiler

Line up a baking sheet with the aluminum foil and place your jalapeno pepper on top of it, with the cut upsides down

Cook Jalapeno peppers for 8 minutes under the broiler until the skin is blackened

Add them to a plastic zip bag

Let the peppers steam off for 20 minutes

Remove them and discard the skin

Blend the jalapeno peppers, onion, beer, strawberry preserve, olive oil, BBQ sauce, sea salt and just a pinch of ground black pepper altogether in a blender until the sauce is fully smoothened out

Transfer the sauce to a container and cover it up with a lid, let it chill for 8 hours or overnight

Pre-heat your oven to about 200 degrees Fahrenheit and cook ribs for about an hour

Increase the temp to 225 degrees Fahrenheit and keep cooking for another 2-3 hours

Preheat your smoker than to a Smoke Temperature of 250 degrees Fahrenheit

Unwrap your cooked ribs and discard away the apple juice

Place them on top of your smoker

Cook on your smoker until the surface of your meat is finely dried up, it should take about 5-10 minutes After which, continue cooking, making sure to brush it up with the sauce after every 15 minutes

Turn it around after 30 minutes

Repeat and cook for 1 hour

Serve hot when tender

Nutrition:

Calories: 169

Fats: 5g

Carbs: 3g

Fiber: 3g

Easy Pork Chuck Roast

Preparation Time: 15 minutes

Cooking Time: 4-5 hours

Servings: 4

Ingredients:

- 1 whole 4-5 pounds chuck roast
- ¼ cup olive oil
- ¼ cup firm packed brown sugar
- 2 tablespoons Cajun seasoning
- 2 tablespoons paprika
- 2 tablespoons cayenne pepper

Directions:

Pre-heat your smoker to 225 degrees Fahrenheit using oak Preferred Wood Pellet

Rub chuck roast all over with olive oil

Take a small bowl and add brown sugar, paprika, Cajun seasoning, cayenne

Coat the roast well with the spice mix

Transfer the chuck roast to smoker rack and smoke for 4-5 hours

Once the internal Smoke Temperature reaches 165 degrees Fahrenheit, take the meat out and slice

Enjoy!

Nutrition:

Calories: 219

Fats: 16g

Carbs: 0g

Fiber: 3g

Jalapeno-Bacon Pork Tenderloin

Preparation Time: 25 minutes

Cooking Time: 2 hours and 30 minutes

Servings: 4 to 6

Ingredients:

- ¼ cup yellow mustard
- 2 (1-pound) pork tenderloins
- ¼ cup Our House Dry Rub
- 8 ounces cream cheese, softened
- 1 cup grated Cheddar cheese
- 1 tablespoon unsalted butter, melted
- 1 tablespoon minced garlic

- 2 jalapeño peppers, seeded and diced
- 1½ pounds bacon

Directions:

Slather the mustard all over the pork tenderloins, then sprinkle generously with the dry rub to coat the meat.

Supply your smoker with Preferred Wood Pellet pellets and follow the manufacturer's specific start-up procedure. Preheat, with the lid closed, to 225°F.

Place the tenderloins directly on the grill, close the lid, and smoke for 2 hours.

Remove the pork from the grill and increase the Smoke Temperature to 375°F.

In a small bowl, combine the cream cheese, Cheddar cheese, melted butter, garlic, and jalapeños.

Starting from the top, slice deeply along the center of each tenderloin end to end, creating a cavity.

Spread half of the cream cheese mixture in the cavity of one tenderloin. Repeat with the remaining mixture and the other piece of meat.

Securely wrap one tenderloin with half of the bacon. Repeat with the remaining bacon and the other piece of meat.

Transfer the bacon-wrapped tenderloins to the grill, close the lid, and smoke for about 30 minutes, or until a meat thermometer inserted in the thickest part of the meat reads 160°F and the bacon is browned and cooked through.

Let the tenderloins rest for 5 to 10 minutes before slicing and serving.

Nutrition:

Calories: 527 kCal

Smoked Brats

Preparation Time: 10 minutes

Cooking Time: 1 hour and 30 minutes- 2 hours

Servings: 10

Ingredients:

- 4 (12-ounce) cans of beer
- 2 onions, sliced into rings
- 2 green bell peppers, sliced into rings
- 2 tablespoons unsalted butter, plus more for the rolls
- 2 tablespoons red pepper flakes
- 10 brats, uncooked
- 10 hoagie rolls, split
- Mustard, for serving

Directions:

On your kitchen stove top, in a large saucepan over high heat, bring the beer, onions, peppers, butter, and red pepper flakes to a boil.

Supply your smoker with Preferred Wood Pellet pellets and follow the manufacturer's specific start-up procedure. Preheat, with the lid closed, to 225°F.

Place a disposable pan on one side of grill, and pour the warmed beer mixture into it, creating a "brat tub" (see Tip below).

Place the brats on the other side of the grill, directly on the grate, and close the lid and smoke for 1 hour, turning 2 or 3 times.

Add the brats to the pan with the onions and peppers, cover tightly with aluminum foil, and continue smoking with the lid closed for 30 minutes to 1 hour, or until a meat thermometer inserted in the brats reads 160°F.

Butter the cut sides of the hoagie rolls and toast cut side down on the grill.

Using a slotted spoon, remove the brats, onions, and peppers from the cooking liquid and discard the liquid.

Serve the brats on the toasted buns, topped with the onions and peppers and mustard (ketchup optional).

Nutrition:

Calories: 337 kCal

Country Pork Roast

Preparation Time: 20 minutes

Cooking Time: 3 hours

Servings: 8

Ingredients:

- 1 (28-ounce) jar or 2 (14.5-ounce) cans sauerkraut
- 3 Granny Smith apples, cored and chopped
- ¾ cup packed light brown sugar
- 3 tablespoons Greek seasoning
- 2 teaspoons dried basil leaves
- Extra-virgin olive oil, for rubbing
- 1 (2- to 2½-pound) pork loin roast

Directions:

Supply your smoker with Preferred Wood Pellet pellets and follow the manufacturer's specific start-up procedure. Preheat, with the lid closed, to 250°F.

In a large bowl, stir together the sauerkraut, chopped apples, and brown sugar.

Spread the sauerkraut-apple mixture in the bottom of a 9-by-13-inch baking dish.

In a small bowl, mix the Greek seasoning and dried basil for the rub.

Oil the pork roast and apply the rub, then place it fat-side up in the baking dish, on top of the sauerkraut.

Transfer the baking dish to the grill, close the lid, and roast the pork for 3 hours, or until a meat thermometer inserted in the thickest part of the meat reads 160°F.

Remove the pork roast from the baking dish and let rest for 5 minutes before slicing.

To serve, divide the sauerkraut-apple mixture among plates and top with the sliced pork.

Nutrition:

Calories: 459 calories

Pickled-Pepper Pork Chops

Preparation Time: 15 minutes

Cooking Time: 45-50 minutes

Servings: 4

Ingredients:

4 (1-inch-thick) pork chops

½ cup pickled jalapeño juice or pickle juice

¼ cup chopped pickled (jarred) jalapeño pepper slices

¼ cup chopped roasted red peppers

¼ cup canned diced tomatoes, well-dra

ined

¼ cup chopped scallions

2 teaspoons poultry seasoning

2 teaspoons salt

2 teaspoons freshly ground black pepper

Directions:

Pour the jalapeño juice into a large container with a lid. Add the pork chops, cover, and marinate in the refrigerator for at least 4 hours or overnight, supplementing with or substituting pickle juice as desired.

In a small bowl, combine the chopped pickled jalapeños, roasted red peppers, tomatoes, scallions, and poultry seasoning to make a relish. Set aside.

Remove the pork chops from the marinade and shake off any excess. Discard the marinade. Season both sides of the chops with the salt and pepper.

Supply your smoker with Preferred Wood Pellet pellets and follow the manufacturer's specific start-up procedure. Preheat, with the lid closed, to 325°F.

Arrange the pork chops directly on the grill, close the lid, and smoke for 45 to 50 minutes, without flipping, until a meat thermometer inserted in the meat reads 160°F.

To serve, divide the chops among plates and top with the pickled pepper relish.

Nutrition:

Calories: 663 kCal

Lamb

Wood Pellet Smoked Lamb Shoulder

Preparation Time: 15 minutes

Cooking Time: 1 hour and 30 minutes

Servings: 7

Ingredients:

For Smoked Lamb Shoulder

- 5 lb. lamb shoulder, boneless and excess fat trimmed
- 2 tbsp kosher salt
- 2 tbsp black pepper

- 1 tbsp rosemary, dried

The Injection

- 1 cup apple cider vinegar

The Spritz

- 1 cup apple cider vinegar
- 1 cup apple juice

Directions:

Preheat the wood pellet smoker with a water pan to 2250 F.

Rinse the lamb in cold water then pat it dry with a paper towel. Inject vinegar to the lamb.

Dry the lamb again and rub with oil, salt black pepper and rosemary. Tie with kitchen twine.

Smoke uncovered for 1 hour then spritz after every 15 minutes until the internal temperature reaches 1950 F.

Remove the lamb from the grill and place it on a platter. Let cool before shredding it and enjoying it with your favorite side.

Nutrition:

Calories: 240; Fat: 19g; Protein: 17g

Wood Pellet Smoked Pulled Lamb Sliders

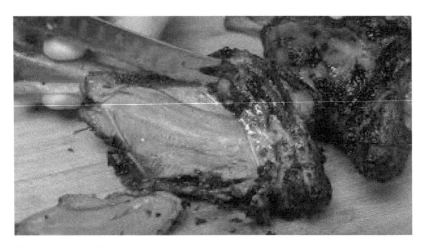

Preparation Time: 10 minutes

Cooking Time: 7 hours

Servings: 7

Ingredients:

- 5 lb. lamb shoulder, boneless
- 1/2 cup olive oil
- 1/4 cup dry rub
- 10 oz spritz

The Dry Rub

- 1/3 cup kosher salt
- 1/3 cup pepper, ground

- 1-1/3 cup garlic, granulated

The Spritz

- 4 oz Worcestershire sauce
- 6 oz apple cider vinegar

Directions:

Preheat the wood pellet smoker with a water bath to 2500 F.

Trim any fat from the lamb then rub with oil and dry rub.

Place the lamb on the smoker for 90 minutes then spritz with a spray bottle every 30 minutes until the internal temperature reaches 1650 F.

Transfer the lamb shoulder to a foil pan with the remaining spritz liquid and cover tightly with foil.

Place back in the smoker and smoke until the internal temperature reaches 2000 F.

Remove from the smoker and let rest for 30 minutes before pulling the lamb and serving with slaw, bun, or aioli. Enjoy.

Nutrition:

Calories: 339; Fat: 22g; Carbs: 16g; Protein: 18g

Smoked Lamb Meatballs

Preparation Time: 10 minutes

Cooking Time: 1 hour

Servings: 5

Ingredients:

- 1 lb. lamb shoulder, ground
- 3 garlic cloves, finely diced
- 3 tbsp shallot, diced
- 1 tbsp salt
- 1 egg
- 1/2 tbsp pepper

- 1/2 tbsp cumin
- 1/2 tbsp smoked paprika
- 1/4 tbsp red pepper flakes
- 1/4 tbsp cinnamon, ground
- 1/4 cup panko breadcrumbs

Directions:

Set the wood pellet smoker to 2500 F using a fruitwood.

In a mixing bowl, combine all meatball ingredients until well mixed.

Form small-sized balls and place them on a baking sheet. Place the baking sheet in the smoker and smoke until the internal temperature reaches 1600 F.

Remove from the smoker and serve. Enjoy.

Nutrition:

Calories: 73

Fat: 5g

Carbs: 2g

Protein: 5g

Crown Rack of Lamb

Preparation Time: 10 minutes

Cooking Time: 30 minutes

Servings: 6

Ingredients:

- 2 racks of lamb, frenched
- 1 tbsp garlic, crushed
- 1 tbsp rosemary, finely chopped
- 1/4 cup olive oil
- 2 feet twine

Directions:

Rinse the racks with cold water then pat them dry with a paper towel.

Lay the racks on a flat board then score between each bone, about ¼ inch down.

In a mixing bowl, mix garlic, rosemary, and oil then generously brush on the lamb.

Take each lamb rack and bend it into a semicircle forming a crown-like shape.

Use the twine to wrap the racks about 4 times starting from the base to the top. Make sure you tie the twine tightly to keep the racks together.

Preheat the wood pellet to 400-4500 F then place the lamb racks on a baking dish.

Cook for 10 minutes then reduce temperature to 3000 F. cook for 20 more minutes or until the internal temperature reaches 1300 F.

Remove the lamb rack from the wood pellet and let rest for 15 minutes.

Serve when hot with veggies and potatoes. Enjoy.

Nutrition:

Calories: 390; Fat: 35g; Protein: 17g

Wood Pellet Smoked Leg of Lamb

Preparation Time: 15 minutes

Cooking Time: 3 hours

Servings: 6

Ingredients:

- 1 leg lamb, boneless
- 4 garlic cloves, minced
- 2 tbsp salt
- 1 tbsp black pepper, freshly ground
- 2 tbsp oregano

- 1 tbsp thyme
- 2 tbsp olive oil

Directions:

Trim any excess fat from the lamb and tie the lamb using twine to form a nice roast.

In a mixing bowl, mix garlic, spices, and oil. Rub all over the lamb, wrap with a plastic bag then refrigerate for an hour to marinate.

Place the lamb on a smoker set at 2500 F. smoke the lamb for 4 hours or until the internal temperature reaches 1450 F.

Remove from the smoker and let rest to cool. Serve and enjoy.

Nutrition:

Calories: 350

Fat: 16g

Carbs: 3g

Protein: 49g

Simple Grilled Lamb Chops

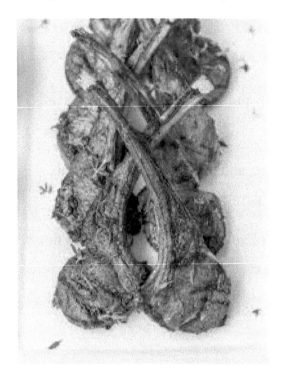

Preparation Time: 10 minutes

Cooking Time: 6 minutes

Servings: 6

Ingredients:

- 1/4 cup distilled white vinegar
- 2 tbsp salt
- 1/2 tbsp black pepper

- 1 tbsp garlic, minced
- 1 onion, thinly sliced
- 2 tbsp olive oil
- 2 lb. lamb chops

Directions:

In a resealable bag, mix vinegar, salt, black pepper, garlic, sliced onion, and oil until all salt has dissolved.

Add the lamb chops and toss until well coated. Place in the fridge to marinate for 2 hours.

Preheat the wood pellet grill to high heat.

Remove the lamb from the fridge and discard the marinade. Wrap any exposed bones with foil.

Grill the lamb for 3 minutes per side. You can also broil in a broiler for more crispness.

Serve and enjoy.

Nutrition:

Calories: 519; Fat: 45g; Carbs: 2g; Protein: 25g

Spicy Chinese Cumin Lamb Skewers

Preparation Time: 20 minutes

Cooking Time: 6 minutes

Servings: 10

Ingredients:

- 1 lb. lamb shoulder, cut into 1/2-inch pieces
- 10 skewers
- 2 tbsp ground cumin
- 2 tbsp red pepper flakes
- 1 tbsp salt

Directions:

Thread the lamb pieces onto skewers.

Preheat the wood pellet grill to medium heat and lightly oil the grill grate.

Place the skewers on the grill grate and cook while turning occasionally. Sprinkle cumin, pepper flakes, and salt every time you turn the skewer.

Cook for 6 minutes or until nicely browned.

Serve and enjoy.

Nutrition:

Calories: 77

Fat: 5g

Carbs: 2g

Protein: 6g

Poultry

Paprika Chicken

Preparation Time: 20 minutes

Cooking Time: 2 – 4 hours

Servings: 7

Ingredients:

- 4-6 chicken breast
- 4 tablespoons olive oil
- 2 tablespoons smoked paprika
- ½ tablespoon salt

- ¼ teaspoon pepper
- 2 teaspoons garlic powder
- 2 teaspoons garlic salt
- 2 teaspoons pepper
- 1 teaspoon cayenne pepper
- 1 teaspoon rosemary

Directions:

Preheat your smoker to 220 degrees Fahrenheit using your favorite wood Pellets

Prepare your chicken breast according to your desired shapes and transfer to a greased baking dish

Take a medium bowl and add spices, stir well

Press the spice mix over chicken and transfer the chicken to smoker

Smoke for 1-1 and a ½ hours

Turn-over and cook for 30 minutes more

Once the internal temperature reaches 165 degrees Fahrenheit

Remove from the smoker and cover with foil

Allow it to rest for 15 minutes

Enjoy!

Nutrition:

Calories: 237

Fats: 6.1g

Carbs: 14g

Fiber: 3g

Citrus Flavored Goose Breast

Preparation Time: 6 hours

Cooking Time: 40 minutes

Servings: 6

Ingredients:

- ½ a cup of orange juice
- 1/3 cup of olive oil
- 1/3 cup of Dijon mustard
- 1/3 cup of brown sugar
- ¼ cup of soy sauce
- ¼ cup of honey
- 1 tablespoon of dried minced onion
- 1 teaspoon of garlic powder

- 8 goose breast halves
- 1 cup of soaked hickory wood chips

Directions:

Take a medium sized bowl and whisk in the orange juice, mustard, olive oil, soy sauce, sugar onion, and honey and garlic powder. Mix the marinade well.

Place the goose in the marinade and cover it up.

Let it refrigerate for about 3-6 hours. Preheat your smoker to a temperature of 300 degrees Fahrenheit. Add some soaked hickory wood chips to create added smoke.

Place the breasts on the grate and brush them up occasionally with the marinade for the first 30 minutes.

Smoke them until the juices run clear and the breast reaches an internal temperature of 165 degrees Fahrenheit.

Nutrition:

Calories: 1094

Protein: 32g

Carbs: 14g

Fat: 64g

Smoked Brown Sugar Turkey

Preparation Time: 15 minutes

Cooking Time: 8 hours

Servings: 6

Ingredients:

- 2 lbs. Turkey breast
- 4 cups Cold water
- ¼ cup Salt
- 1 cup Brown sugar
- 2 tbsp. Garlic powder
- 1 tbsp. Sea salt
- 1 tbsp. Cayenne pepper

- 2 tbsp. dried onions
- 2 tbsps. Sugar
- 2 tbsps. Chili powder
- 2 tbsps. Black pepper
- 2 tbsps. Cumin
- ¼ cup Paprika
- 2 tbsps. Brown sugar

Directions:

In a large enough bowl, mix together all of the brine ingredients except the turkey.

Add the turkey and cover with brine properly. Put this bowl in your refrigerator for about 15–20 hours.

Remove the turkey from the mixture of brine.

Prepare your Wood Pellet Smoker-Grill by preheating it to a temperature of about 180°F. Close the lid for about 15 minutes before adding the turkey.

Prepare the BBQ rub with the provided ingredients and coat the turkey properly.

Transfer this seasoned turkey straight to the grilling grate.

Allow for about 6–8 hours of smoking to get an internal temperature of about 160°F.

Remove the smoked turkey from your smoker-grill and allow it to rest for at least 10 minutes.

Nutrition:

Calories: 155

Protein: 29g

Carbs: 8g

Fat: 3g

Sweet Smoked Gingery Lemon Chicken

Preparation Time: 30 minutes

Cooking Time: 6hours

Servings: 1

Ingredients:

- Whole chicken 2 (4-lbs., 1.8-kgs)
- Olive oil – ¼ cup
- The Rub
- Salt – ¼ cup
- Pepper – 2 tablespoons
- Garlic powder – ¼ cup

The Filling

- Fresh Ginger – 8, 1-inch each
- Cinnamon sticks – 8
- Sliced lemon – ½ cup
- Cloves - 6

The Smoke

Preheat the smoker an hour prior to smoking.

Add soaked hickory wood chips during the smoking time.

Directions:

Preheat a smoker to 225°F (107°C). Use soaked hickory wood chips to make indirect heat.

Rub the chicken with salt, pepper, and garlic powder then set aside.

Fill the chicken cavities with ginger, cinnamon sticks, cloves, and sliced lemon then brush olive oil all over the chicken.

When the smoker is ready, place the whole chicken on the smoker's rack.

Smoke the whole chicken for 4 hours then check whether the internal temperature has reached 160°F (71°C).

When the chicken is done, remove the smoked chicken from the smoker then let it warm for a few minutes.

Serve and enjoy right away or cut into slices.

Nutrition:

Carbohydrates: 27 g

Protein: 19 g

Sodium: 65 mg

Cholesterol: 49 mg

Buffalo Chicken Thighs

Preparation Time: 30 minutes

Cooking Time: 6hours

Servings: 1

Ingredients:

- 4-6 skinless, boneless chicken thighs
- Traeger Pork and poultry rub
- 4 tablespoons of butter
- 1 cup of sauce; buffalo wing
- Bleu cheese crumbles
- Ranch dressing

Directions:

Set the grill to preheat by keeping the temperature to 450 degrees F and keeping the lid closed

Now season the chicken thighs with the poultry rub and then place it on the grill grate

Cook it for 8 to 10 minutes while making sure to flip it once midway

Now take a small saucepan and cook the wing sauce along with butter by keeping the flame on medium heat. Make sure to stir in between to avoid lumps

Now take the cooked chicken and dip it into the wing sauce and the butter mix. Make sure to coat both the sides in an even manner

Take the chicken thighs that have been sauced to the grill and then cook for further 15 minutes. Do so until the internal temperature reads 175 degrees

Sprinkle bleu cheese and drizzle the ranch dressing

Serve and enjoy

Nutrition:

Carbohydrates: 29 g

Protein: 19 g

Sodium: 25 mg

Smoked Whole Chicken with Honey Glaze

Preparation Time: 30 minutes

Cooking Time: 3hours

Servings: 1

Ingredients:

- 1 4 pounds of chicken with the giblets thoroughly removed and patted dry
- 1 ½ lemon
- 1 tablespoon of honey
- 4 tablespoons of unsalted butter

- 4 tablespoon of chicken seasoning

Directions

Fire up your smoker and set the temperature to 225 degrees F

Take a small saucepan and melt the butter along with honey over a low flame

Now squeeze ½ lemon in this mixture and then move it from the heat source

Take the chicken and smoke by keeping the skin side down. Do so until the chicken turns light brown and the skin starts to release from the grate.

Turn the chicken over and apply the honey butter mixture to it

Continue to smoke it making sure to taste it every 45 minutes until the thickest core reaches a temperature of 160 degrees F

Now remove the chicken from the grill and let it rest for 5 minutes

Serve with the leftover sliced lemon and enjoy

Nutrition:

Carbohydrates: 29 g

Protein: 19 g

Chicken Cordon Bleu

Preparation Time: 15 minutes

Cooking Time: 40 minutes

Servings: 6

Ingredients:

- 6 boneless skinless chicken breasts
- 6 slices of ham
- 12 slices swiss cheese
- 1 cup panko breadcrumbs
- ½ cup all-purpose flour
- 1 tsp ground black pepper or to taste
- 1 tsp salt or to taste

- 4 tbsp grated parmesan cheese
- 2 tbsp melted butter
- ½ tsp garlic powder
- ½ tsp thyme
- ¼ tsp parsley

Directions:

Butterfly the chicken breast with a pairing knife. Place the chicken breast in between 2 plastic wraps and pound with a mallet until the chicken breasts are ¼ inch thick.

Place a plastic wrap on a flat surface. Place one fat chicken breast on it.

Place one slice of swiss cheese on the chicken. Place one slice of ham over the cheese and place another cheese slice over the ham.

Roll the chicken breast tightly. Fold both ends of the roll tightly. Pin both ends of the rolled chicken breast with a toothpick.

Repeat step 3 and 4 for the remaining chicken breasts

In a mixing bowl, combine the all-purpose flour, ½ tsp salt, and ½ tsp pepper. Set aside.

In another mixing bowl, combine breadcrumbs, parmesan, butter, garlic, thyme, parsley, ½ tsp salt, and ½ tsp pepper. Set aside.

Break the eggs into another mixing bowl and whisk. Set aside.

Grease a baking sheet.

Bake one chicken breast roll. Dip into the flour mixture, brush with eggs and dip into breadcrumb mixture. The chicken breast should be coated.

Place it on the baking sheet.

Repeat steps 9 and 10 for the remaining breast rolls.

Preheat your grill to 375°F with the lid closed for 15 minutes.

Place the baking sheet on the grill and cook for about 40 minutes, or until the chicken is golden brown.

Remove the baking sheet from the grill and let the chicken rest for a few minutes.

Slice cordon bleu and serve.

Nutrition:

Calories: 560

Total Fat:: 27.4 g

Total Carbohydrate: 23.2 g

Protein: 54.3 g

Seafood

Sweet Grilled Lobster Tails

Preparation Time: 10 minutes

Cooking Time: 7 minutes

Servings: 12

Ingredients:

- 12 lobster tails
- ½ C olive oil
- ¼ C fresh lemon juice
- ½ C butter
- 1 Tbsp. crushed garlic
- 1 tsp sugar
- 1/2 tsp salt
- ½ tsp black pepper

Directions:

Combine lemon juice, butter, garlic, salt, and pepper over med-low heat and mix until well blended, keep warm.

Create a "cool zone" at one end of the pellet grill. Brush the meat side of tails with olive oil, place onto grill and cook for 5-7 minutes, depending on the size of the lobster tail.

Make sure to turn once during cooking process.

After turning, baste meat with garlic butter 2-3 times.

The shell should be bright red when they are finished. Remove the tails from the grill, and using large kitchen shears, cut the top part of the shell open.

Serve with warm garlic butter for dipping.

Nutrition:

Calories 208

Total Fat 10g

Saturated Fat 6g

Unsaturated Fat 4g

Cholesterol 99mg

Seasoned Smoked Oysters

Preparation Time: 20 minutes

Cooking Time: 1½-2 hours

Servings: 2 dozen

Ingredients:

- 1-gallon cold water
- ½ cup soy sauce
- 2 tablespoons Worcestershire sauce
- 1 cup salt
- 1 cup firmly packed brown sugar
- 2 dried bay leaves
- 2 garlic cloves, minced
- 2 teaspoons freshly ground black pepper
- 1 tablespoon hot sauce
- 1 tablespoon onion powder
- 2 dozen raw, shucked oysters, shells discarded
- ¼ cup olive oil
- ½ cup (1 stick) unsalted butter, at room Smoke Temperature
- 1 teaspoon garlic powder
- Crackers or toast points, for serving
- Cocktail sauce, for serving

Directions:

In a large container, mix the water, soy sauce, Worcestershire, salt, sugar, bay leaves, garlic, pepper, hot sauce, and onion powder.

Submerge the raw oysters in the brine, cover the container, and refrigerate overnight.

Following the manufacturer's specific start-up procedure, preheat the smoker to 225°F, and add alder, hickory, or oak Preferred Wood Pellet.

Remove the oysters from the refrigerator, discarding the brine, and rinse them well.

Place the oysters on a nonstick grill mat, drizzle with the olive oil, and place the mat in the smoker.

Smoke the oysters for 1½ to 2 hours, until firm. Meanwhile, in a small bowl, stir together the butter and garlic powder.

Remove the oysters from Preferred Wood Pellet, and drizzle with the seasoned butter.

Serve the oysters with the crackers or toast points and cocktail sauce.

Nutrition:

Calories: 57

Carbs: 13g

Fat: 0.2g

Protein: 3g

Sugar-Crusted Red Snapper

Preparation Time: 10 minutes

Cooking Time: 1 TO 1½ hours

Servings: 2

Ingredients:

- 1 tablespoon brown sugar
- 2 teaspoons minced garlic
- 2 teaspoons salt
- 2 teaspoons freshly ground black pepper
- ½ teaspoon crushed red pepper flakes
- 1 (1½- to 2-pound) red snapper fillet
- 2 tablespoons olive oil, plus more for oiling the grate
- 1 sliced lime, for garnish

Directions:

Following the manufacturer's specific start-up procedure, preheat the smoker to 225°F, and add alder Preferred Wood Pellet.

In a small bowl, mix the brown sugar, garlic, and salt, pepper, and red pepper flakes to make a spice blend.

Rub the olive oil all over the fish and apply the spice blend to coat.

Oil the grill grate or a nonstick grill mat or perforated pizza screen. Place the fillet on the smoker rack and smoke for 1 to 1½ hours, until the internal Smoke Temperature registers 145°F.

Remove the fish from Preferred Wood Pellet and serve hot with the lime slices.

Nutrition:

Calories: 57

Carbs: 13g

Fat: 0.2g

Fiber: 6g

Protein: 3g

Peppercorn-Dill Mahi-Mahi

Preparation Time: 10 minutes

Cooking Time: 1 to 1½ hours

Servings: 4

Ingredients:

4 mahi-mahi fillets

¼ cup chopped fresh dill

2 tablespoons freshly squeezed lemon juice

1 tablespoon crushed black peppercorns

2 teaspoons minced garlic

1 teaspoon onion powder

1 teaspoon salt

2 tablespoons olive oil, plus more for oiling the grate

Directions:

Following the manufacturer's specific start-up procedure, preheat the smoker to 225°F, and add alder or pecan Preferred Wood Pellet.

Trim the fillets as needed, cutting out any visible red bloodline. It will not hurt you, but its stronger flavor can quickly permeate the rest of the fillet.

In a small bowl, whisk together the dill, lemon juice, peppercorns, garlic, onion powder, and salt to make a seasoning.

Rub the fish with the olive oil and apply the seasoning all over. Oil the grill grate or a nonstick grill mat or perforated pizza screen.

Place the fillets on the smoker rack and smoke for 1 to 1½ hours, until the flesh is opaque and the internal Smoke Temperature registers 145°F.

Remove the fillets from Preferred Wood Pellet and serve hot.

Nutrition:

Calories: 57

Carbs: 13g

Fat: 0.2g

Fiber: 6g

Protein: 3g

Fish Tacos with Sweet and Fiery Peppers

Preparation Time: 15 minutes

Cooking Time: 1 hour

Servings: 4

Ingredients:

- 1 (16-ounce) carton prepared sweet coleslaw
- 1 small red onion, chopped
- 1 poblano pepper, chopped
- 1 jalapeño pepper, chopped
- 1 serrano pepper, chopped
- ¼ cup chopped fresh cilantro
- 1 tablespoon minced garlic
- 2 teaspoons salt, divided
- 2 teaspoons freshly ground black pepper, divided
- 1 lime, halved
- 1-pound skinless cod, halibut, or any white fish (see tip)
- 1 tablespoon olive oil, plus more for oiling the grate
- Flour or corn tortillas
- 1 avocado, sliced thin

Directions:

In a medium bowl, stir together the coleslaw, onion, poblano, jalapeño, serrano, cilantro, garlic, and 1 teaspoon each of salt and pepper to make a sweet hot-pepper slaw. Refrigerate the slaw until ready to serve.

Following the manufacturer's specific start-up procedure, preheat the smoker to 225°F, and add apricot or alder Preferred Wood Pellet.

Juice one half of the lime and cut the other half into wedges.

Rub the fish all over with the lime juice and olive oil.

Season the fish with the remaining 1 teaspoon each of salt and pepper. Oil the grill grate or a nonstick grill mat or perforated pizza screen.

Place the fish on the smoker rack and smoke for 1 to 1½ hours

Five to 10 minutes before the end of the cook, place the tortillas on a damp paper towel. Wrap the tortillas in heavy-duty aluminum foil with the towel. Seal the foil tightly and place on the smoker rack.

Remove the fish and tortillas from Preferred Wood Pellet when the fish is flaky and opaque and the internal Smoke Temperature registers 145°F.

Cut the fish into small chunks. Serve the fish pieces with the tortillas, avocado slices, and sweet hot-pepper slaw.

Nutrition:

Calories: 57

Carbs: 13g

Fat: 0.2g

Fiber: 6g

Protein: 3g

Honey-Cayenne Sea Scallops

Preparation Time: 10 minutes

Cooking Time: 25 minutes

Servings: 4

Ingredients:

- ½ cup (1 stick) butter, melted
- ¼ cup honey
- 2 tablespoons ground cayenne pepper
- 1 tablespoon brown sugar
- 1 teaspoon garlic powder
- 1 teaspoon onion powder
- ½ teaspoon salt
- 20 sea scallops (about 2 pounds)

Directions:

Following the manufacturer's specific start-up procedure, preheat the smoker to 225°F, and add oak or cherry Preferred Wood Pellet.

In a small bowl, whisk together the butter, honey, cayenne, brown sugar, garlic powder, onion powder, and salt.

Place the scallops in a disposable aluminum foil roasting pan and pour the seasoned honey butter over them.

Set the pan on the smoker rack and smoke the scallops for about 25 minutes, until opaque and firm and the internal Smoke Temperature registers 130°F.

Remove the scallops from Preferred Wood Pellet and serve hot.

Nutrition:

Calories: 57

Carbs: 13g

Fat: 0.2g

Fiber: 6g

Protein: 3g

Lemon Butter Lobster Tails

Preparation Time: 30 minutes

Cooking Time: 45 minutes -1 hour

Servings: 4

Ingredients:

- 4 (8-ounce) lobster tails, fresh (not frozen)
- 1 cup (2 sticks) unsalted butter, melted, divided
- Juice of 2 lemons
- 1 teaspoon minced garlic
- 1 teaspoon dried thyme
- 1 teaspoon dried rosemary
- 1 teaspoon salt
- 1 teaspoon freshly ground black pepper
- Olive oil, for oiling the grate
- ¼ cup chopped fresh parsley

Directions:

Following the manufacturer's specific start-up procedure, preheat the smoker to 225°F, and add oak or alder Preferred Wood Pellet.

Split the top of each tail: Grasp the shell and lift it up. Using strong kitchen shears, cut down the middle of the shell, front to back, to the last tail segment. Gently lift the front end of the meat from the shell and rest it on the split shell, leaving the base of the tail attached. Open and rinse out any existing grit before smoking.

Cut a slit down the center of the meat to open it up slightly.

In a small bowl, whisk together the butter, lemon juice, garlic, thyme, rosemary, salt, and pepper. Baste each lobster tail with 1 tablespoon of lemon butter.

Oil the grill grate or a nonstick grill mat or perforated pizza screen. Place the tails on the smoker rack split-side up.

Smoke the tails for 45 minutes to 1 hour, basting each with 1 tablespoon of lemon butter once during cooking.

Remove the lobster tails from Preferred Wood Pellet when opaque and firm and the internal Smoke Temperature registers 130°F to 140°F.

Sprinkle the lobster tails with the parsley and serve with the remaining lemon butter for dipping.

Nutrition:

Calories: 57

Carbs: 13g

Fat: 0.2g

Protein: 3g

Vegetables

Roasted Okra

Preparation Time: 10 minutes

Cooking Time: 30 minutes

Servings: 4

Ingredients:

- 1-pound whole okra
- 2 tablespoons extra-virgin olive oil
- 2 teaspoons seasoned salt
- 2 teaspoons freshly ground black pepper

Directions:

Supply your smoker with wood pellets and follow the manufacturer's specific start-up procedure. Preheat, with the lid closed, to 400°F. Alternatively, preheat your oven to 400°F.

Line a shallow rimmed baking pan with aluminum foil and coat with cooking spray.

Arrange the okra on the pan in a single layer. Drizzle with the olive oil, turning to coat. Season on all sides with the salt and pepper.

Place the baking pan on the grill grate, close the lid, and smoke for 30 minutes, or until crisp and slightly charred. Alternatively, roast in the oven for 30 minutes.

Serve hot.

Smoking Tip: Whether you make this okra in the oven or in your wood pellet grill, be sure to fully preheat the oven or cook chamber for the best results.

Nutrition:

Calories: 150

Carbohydrates: 15 g

Protein: 79 g

Sodium: 45 mg

Cholesterol: 49 mg

Sweet Potato Chips

Preparation Time: 10 minutes

Cooking Time: 12 to 15 minutes

Servings: 4

Ingredients:

- 2 sweet potatoes
- 1-quart warm water
- 1 tablespoon cornstarch, plus 2 teaspoons
- ¼ cup extra-virgin olive oil
- 1 tablespoon salt
- 1 tablespoon packed brown sugar
- 1 teaspoon ground cinnamon
- 1 teaspoon freshly ground black pepper
- ½ teaspoon cayenne pepper

Directions:

Using a mandoline, thinly slice the sweet potatoes.

Pour the warm water into a large bowl and add 1 tablespoon of cornstarch and the potato slices. Let soak for 15 to 20 minutes.

Supply your smoker with wood pellets and follow the manufacturer's specific start-up procedure. Preheat, with the lid closed, to 375°F.

Drain the potato slices, then arrange in a single layer on a perforated pizza pan or a baking sheet lined with aluminum foil. Brush the potato slices on both sides with the olive oil.

In a small bowl, whisk together the salt, brown sugar, cinnamon, black pepper, cayenne pepper, and the remaining 2 teaspoons of cornstarch. Sprinkle this seasoning blend on both sides of the potatoes.

Place the pan or baking sheet on the grill grate, close the lid, and smoke for 35 to 45 minutes, flipping after 20 minutes, until the chips curl up and become crispy.

Store in an airtight container.

Ingredient Tip: Avoid storing your sweet potatoes in the refrigerator's produce bin, which tends to give them a hard center and an unpleasant flavor. What, you don't have a root cellar? Just keep them in a cool, dry area of your kitchen.

Nutrition:

Calories: 150

Carbohydrates: 15 g

Protein: 79 g

Broccoli-Cauliflower Salad

Preparation Time: 10 minutes

Cooking Time: 12 to 25 minutes

Servings: 4

Ingredients:

- 1½ cups mayonnaise
- ½ cup sour cream
- ¼ cup sugar
- 1 bunch broccoli, cut into small pieces
- 1 head cauliflower, cut into small pieces
- 1 small red onion, chopped
- 6 slices bacon, cooked and crumbled (precooked bacon works well)
- 1 cup shredded Cheddar cheese

Directions:

In a small bowl, whisk together the mayonnaise, sour cream, and sugar to make a dressing.

In a large bowl, combine the broccoli, cauliflower, onion, bacon, and Cheddar cheese.

Pour the dressing over the vegetable mixture and toss well to coat.

Serve the salad chilled.

Ingredient Tip: I like using precooked bacon for barbecue recipes. First of all, it saves a lot of time; second of all, grilling bacon is just a pain.

Nutrition:

Calories: 150

Carbohydrates: 15 g

Protein: 79 g

Sodium: 45 mg

Cholesterol: 49 mg

Bunny Dogs with Sweet and Spicy Jalapeño Relish

Preparation Time: 10 minutes

Cooking Time: 12 to 14 minutes

Servings: 5

Ingredients:

- 8 hot dog-size carrots, peeled
- ¼ cup honey
- ¼ cup yellow mustard
- Nonstick cooking spray or butter, for greasing
- Salt
- Freshly ground black pepper
- 8 hot dog buns
- Sweet and Spicy Jalapeño Relish

Directions:

Prepare the carrots by removing the stems and slicing in half lengthwise.

In a small bowl, whisk together the honey and mustard.

Supply your smoker with wood pellets and follow the manufacturer's specific start-up procedure. Preheat, with the lid closed, to 375°F.

Line a baking sheet with aluminum foil and coat with cooking spray.

Brush the carrots on both sides with the honey mustard and season with salt and pepper; put on the baking sheet.

Place the baking sheet on the grill grate, close the lid, and smoke for 35 to 40 minutes, or until tender and starting to brown.

To serve, lightly toast the hot dog buns on the grill and top each with two slices of carrot and some relish.

Smoking Tip: Be sure to fully preheat your smoker to the temperature called for before placing carrots (or any roasting vegetables) on the grill.

Nutrition:

Calories: 150

Carbohydrates: 15 g

Protein: 79 g

Sodium: 45 mg

Cholesterol: 49 mg

Brussels Sprout Bites with Cilantro-Balsamic Drizzle

Preparation Time: 10 minutes

Cooking Time: 12 to 50 minutes

Servings: 4

Ingredients:

- 1-pound Brussels sprouts, trimmed and wilted, leaves removed
- ½ pound bacon, cut in half
- 1 tablespoon packed brown sugar
- 1 tablespoon Cajun seasoning
- ¼ cup balsamic vinegar
- ¼ cup extra-virgin olive oil
- ¼ cup chopped fresh cilantro
- 2 teaspoons minced garlic

Directions:

Soak the toothpicks in water for 15 minutes.

Supply your smoker with wood pellets and follow the manufacturer's specific start-up procedure. Preheat, with the lid closed, to 300°F.

Wrap each Brussels sprout in a half slice of bacon and secure with a toothpick.

In a small bowl, combine the brown sugar and Cajun seasoning. Dip each wrapped Brussels sprout in this sweet rub and roll around to coat.

Place the sprouts on a Frogmat or parchment paper–lined baking sheet on the grill grate, close the lid, and smoke for 45 minutes to 1 hour, turning as needed, until cooked evenly and the bacon is crisp.

In a small bowl, whisk together the balsamic vinegar, olive oil, cilantro, and garlic.

Remove the toothpicks from the Brussels sprouts, transfer to a plate and serve drizzled with the cilantro-balsamic sauce.

Ingredient Tip: When fully cooked, Brussels sprouts often emit a sulfur-like smell—just another great reason to cook outdoors!

Nutrition:

Calories: 150

Carbohydrates: 15 g

Protein: 79 g

Sodium: 45 mg

Smokey Roasted Cauliflower

Preparation Time: 10 minutes

Cooking Time: 1 hour 20 minutes

Servings: 4 to 6

Ingredients:

- 1 head cauliflower
- 1 cup parmesan cheese
- Spice Ingredients:
- 1 tbsp olive oil
- 2 cloves garlic, chopped
- 1 tsp kosher salt
- 1 tsp smoked paprika

Directions:

Preheat pellet grill to 180°F. If applicable, set smoke setting to high.

Cut cauliflower into bite-size flowerets and place in a grill basket. Place basket on the grill grate and smoke for an hour.

Mix spice ingredients. In a small bowl while the cauliflower is smoking. Remove cauliflower from the grill after an hour and let cool.

Change grill temperature to 425°F. After the cauliflower has cooled, put cauliflower in a resealable bag, and pour marinade in the bag. Toss to combine in the bag.

Place cauliflower back in a grill basket and return to grill. Roast in the grill basket for 10-12 minutes or until the outsides begin to get crispy and golden brown.

Remove from grill and transfer to a serving dish. Sprinkle parmesan cheese over the cauliflower and rest for a few minutes so the cheese can melt. Serve and enjoy!

Nutrition:

Calories: 70

Fat: 35 g

Cholesterol: 0

Carbohydrate: 7 g

Fiber: 3 g

Sugar: 3 g

Protein: 3 g

Desserts

Grilled Pineapple with Chocolate Sauce

Preparation Time: 10 minutes

Cooking Time: 25 minutes

Servings: 6 to 8

Ingredients:

- 1 pineapple
- 8 oz bittersweet chocolate chips
- 1/2 cup spiced rum
- 1/2 cup whipping cream
- 2 tbsp light brown sugar

Directions:

Preheat pellet grill to 400°F.

De-skin the pineapple and slice pineapple into 1 in cubes.

In a saucepan, combine chocolate chips. When chips begin to melt, add rum to the saucepan. Continue to stir until combined, then add a splash of the pineapple's juice.

Add in whipping cream and continue to stir the mixture. Once the sauce is smooth and thickening, lower heat to simmer to keep warm.

Thread pineapple cubes onto skewers. Sprinkle skewers with brown sugar.

Place skewers on the grill grate. Grill for about 5 minutes per side, or until grill marks begin to develop.

Remove skewers from grill and allow to rest on a plate for about 5 minutes. Serve alongside warm chocolate sauce for dipping.

Nutrition:

Calories: 112.6

Fat: 0.5 g

Cholesterol: 0

Carbohydrate: 28.8 g

Fiber: 1.6 g

Sugar: 0.1 g

Protein: 0.4 g

Nectarine and Nutella Sundae

Preparation Time: 10 minutes

Cooking Time: 25 minutes

Servings: 4

Ingredients:

- 2 nectarines, halved and pitted
- 2 tsp honey
- 4 tbsp Nutella
- 4 scoops vanilla ice cream
- 1/4 cup pecans, chopped
- Whipped cream, to top
- 4 cherries, to top

Directions:

Preheat pellet grill to 400°F.

Slice nectarines in half and remove the pits.

Brush the inside (cut side) of each nectarine half with honey.

Place nectarines directly on the grill grate, cut side down. Cook for 5-6 minutes, or until grill marks develop.

Flip nectarines and cook on the other side for about 2 minutes.

Remove nectarines from the grill and allow it to cool.

Fill the pit cavity on each nectarine half with 1 tbsp Nutella.

Place 1 scoop of ice cream on top of Nutella. Top with whipped cream, cherries, and sprinkle chopped pecans. Serve and enjoy!

Nutrition:

Calories: 90

Fat: 3 g

Cholesterol: 0

Carbohydrate: 15g

Fiber: 0

Sugar: 13 g

Protein: 2 g

Cinnamon Sugar Donut Holes

Preparation Time: 10 minutes

Cooking Time: 35 minutes

Servings: 4

Ingredients:

- 1/2 cup flour
- 1 tbsp cornstarch
- 1/2 tsp baking powder
- 1/8 tsp baking soda
- 1/8 tsp ground cinnamon
- 1/2 tsp kosher salt
- 1/4 cup buttermilk
- 1/4 cup sugar
- 1 1/2 tbsp butter, melted
- 1 egg
- 1/2 tsp vanilla

Topping Ingredients:

- 2 tbsp sugar
- 1 tbsp sugar
- 1 tsp ground cinnamon

Directions:

Preheat pellet grill to 350°F.

In a medium bowl, combine flour, cornstarch, baking powder, baking soda, ground cinnamon, and kosher salt. Whisk to combine.

In a separate bowl, combine buttermilk, sugar, melted butter, egg, and vanilla. Whisk until the egg is thoroughly combined.

Pour wet mixture into the flour mixture and stir. Stir just until combined, careful not to overwork the mixture.

Spray mini muffin tin with cooking spray.

Spoon 1 tbsp of donut mixture into each mini muffin hole.

Place the tin on the pellet grill grate and bake for about 18 minutes, or until a toothpick can come out clean.

Remove muffin tin from the grill and let rest for about 5 minutes.

In a small bowl, combine 1 tbsp sugar and 1 tsp ground cinnamon.

Melt 2 tbsp of butter in a glass dish. Dip each donut hole in the melted butter, then mix and toss with cinnamon sugar. Place completed donut holes on a plate to serve.

Nutrition:

Calories: 190

Fat: 17 g

Cholesterol: 0

Carbohydrate: 21 g

Fiber: 1 g

Sugar: 8 g

Protein: 3 g

Pellet Grill Chocolate Chip Cookies

Preparation Time: 20 minutes

Cooking Time: 45 minutes

Servings: 12

Ingredients:

- 1 cup salted butter, softened
- 1 cup of sugar
- 1 cup light brown sugar
- 2 tsp vanilla extract
- 2 large eggs
- 3 cups all-purpose flour
- 1 tsp baking soda
- 1/2 tsp baking powder
- 1 tsp natural sea salt
- 2 cups semi-sweet chocolate chips, or chunks

Directions:

Preheat pellet grill to 375°F.

Line a large baking sheet with parchment paper and set aside.

In a medium bowl, mix flour, baking soda, salt, and baking powder. Once combined, set aside.

In stand mixer bowl, combine butter, white sugar, and brown sugar until combined. Beat in eggs and vanilla. Beat until fluffy.

Mix in dry ingredients, continue to stir until combined.

Add chocolate chips and mix thoroughly.

Roll 3 tbsp of dough at a time into balls and place them on your cookie sheet. Evenly space them apart, with about 2-3 inches in between each ball.

Place cookie sheet directly on the grill grate and bake for 20-25 minutes, until the outside of the cookies is slightly browned.

Remove from grill and allow to rest for 10 minutes. Serve and enjoy!

Nutrition:

Calories: 120

Fat: 4

Carbohydrate: 22.8 g

Sugar: 14.4 g

Protein: 1.4 g

Delicious Donuts on a Grill

Preparation Time: 5 minutes

Cooking Time: 10 minutes

Servings: 6

Ingredients:

- 1-1/2 cups sugar, powdered
- 1/3 cup whole milk
- 1/2 teaspoon vanilla extract
- 16 ounces of biscuit dough, prepared
- Oil spray, for greasing
- 1 cup chocolate sprinkles, for sprinkling

Directions:

Take a medium bowl and mix sugar, milk, and vanilla extract.

Combine well to create a glaze.

Set the glaze aside for further use.

Place the dough onto the flat, clean surface.

Flat the dough with a rolling pin.

Use a ring mold, about an inch, and cut the hole in the center of each round dough.

Place the dough on a plate and refrigerate for 10 minutes.

Open the grill and install the grill grate inside it.

Close the hood.

Now, select the grill from the menu, and set the temperature to medium.

Set the time to 6 minutes.

Select start and begin preheating.

Remove the dough from the refrigerator and coat it with cooking spray from both sides.

When the unit beeps, the grill is preheated; place the adjustable amount of dough on the grill grate.

Close the hood, and cook for 3 minutes.

After 3 minutes, remove donuts and place the remaining dough inside.

Cook for 3 minutes.

Once all the donuts are ready, sprinkle chocolate sprinkles on top.

Enjoy.

Nutrition:

Calories: 400

Total Fat: 11g

Saturated Fat: 4.2g

Cholesterol: 1mg

Sodium: 787mg

Total Carbohydrate: 71.3g

Dietary Fiber 0.9g

Total Sugars: 45.3g

Protein: 5.7g

Rubs and Sauces

Carolina Barbeque Rub

Preparation Time: 5 minutes

Cooking Time: 5 minutes

Servings: 1

Ingredients:

- 2 tbsp. Salt
- 2 tbsp. ground Black pepper
- 2 tbsp. White sugar
- ¼ cup Paprika
- 2 tbsp. Brown sugar
- 2 tbsp. ground Cumin
- 2 tbsp. Chili powder

Directions:

Simply place all ingredients into an airtight jar, stir well to combine then close.

Use within six months.

Nutrition:

Calories: 50

Fat: 0.5g

Carbs: 10g

Protein: 1g

Memphis Rub

Preparation Time: 5 minutes

Cooking Time: 5 minutes

Servings: 1

Ingredients:

- ½ cup (55g) paprika
- ¼ cup (40g) garlic powder
- ¼ cup (30g) mild chili powder
- 3 tbsp. salt
- 3 tbsp. black pepper
- 2 tbsp. onion powder
- 2 tbsp. celery seeds
- 1 tbsp. brown sugar
- 1 tbsp. dried oregano
- 1 tbsp. dried thyme
- 1 tbsp. cumin
- 2 tsp. dry mustard
- 2 tsp. ground coriander
- 2 tsp. ground allspice

Directions:

Simply place all ingredients into an airtight jar, stir well to combine then close.

Use within six months.

Nutrition:

Calories: 50

Fat: 0.3g

Carbs: 13g

Protein: 1g

Smoked Soy Sauce

Preparation Time: 15 minutes

Cooking Time: 1 hour

Servings: 1

Ingredients:

- 100ml soy sauce
- Bradley flavor bisquettes cherry

Directions:

Put soy sauce in a heat-resistant bowl, large-mouth. Smoke in a smoker at 158-176 F for about 1 hour. Stir a few times. Remove and cool then put in a bottle. Let sit for one day.

Serve and enjoy!

Nutrition:

Calories 110

Fat 0g

Carbs 25g,

Protein 2g

Smoked Garlic Sauce

Preparation Time: 5 minutes

Cooking Time: 30 minutes

Servings: 2

Ingredients:

- 3 whole garlic heads
- 1/2 cup mayonnaise
- 1/4 cup sour cream
- 2 tbsp. lemon juice
- 2 tbsp. cider vinegar
- Salt to taste

Directions:

Cut the garlic heads off then place in a microwave-safe bowl; add 2 tbsp. water and cover. Microwave for about 5-6 minutes on medium.

Heat your grill on medium. Place the garlic heads in a shallow 'boat' foil and smoke for about 20-25 minutes until soft.

Transfer the garlic heads into a blender. Process for a few minutes until smooth. Add remaining ingredients and process until everything is combined.

Enjoy!

Nutrition:

Calories 20

Fat 0g

Carbs 10g

Protein 0g

Conclusion

These days, anyone can own a pellet grill since manufacturers meet clients' demands from various backgrounds. Since buying a pellet smoker, you need wood pellets to make your grilling process enjoyable. In this Wood Pellet Smoker & Grill Cookbook, you learned everything you have to know about Wood Pellet Smoker & Grill; you learned how to use your Wood Pellet Smoker & Grill to its full potential. Whether you're an amateur home cook hosting a backyard cookout or a pitmaster at a barbecue competition, a Wood Pellet Smoker & Grill can easily become one of the most important appliances you can own to help you make flavorful meals with much less effort.

This cookbook has helped you solve all your pellet grill problems. It is a one-of-a-kind cookbook for those who have a pellet grill and want specific food recipes. If you own a smoker, this book is just right for you. Cooking with a Wood Pellet Smoker & Grill allows you to choose the desired flavor of wood pellets to create the perfect smoke to flavor your food. Each wood pellet type has its personality and taste. The best part is you can use a single flavor or experiment to mix and match the flavors to invent your own combination. Fantastic for making smoked foods or desserts, where a taste is the only character required.

To make perfect wood smoke, you need to find a Wood Pellet Smoker & Grill to fit your cooking needs. For people in the kitchen for a long time, it is hard to get used to a new cooking utensil. It is much easier to get in and figure out a new system rather than learning a new technique. However, if you are looking to explore cooking and new methods, a Wood Pellet Smoker & Grill might be the right choice for you–somebody who wants to take advantage of the increased popularity of Wood Pellet Smoker & Grill!

Now that you know how to smoke meats with your cooking style, it's time to make things interesting in your home. They can't get enough of your smoked pork ribs, and they can't wait for you to introduce the next play of your grilling strategies. If you have been thinking of firing up your Wood Pellet Smoker & Grill, it's time to play out your imagination. The things you'll be making will surely surprise them.

Cooking isn't a hobby; it's a lifestyle where you have a healthy existence in your own way. Make sure that you can cook everything from meat to veggies to different types of fruit. Be true to your family and be sure not to serve them unhealthy meals every chance you get. Make them a big, happy family by giving them delicious eats.

In this cookbook, you've gained all knowledge and mouthwatering recipes to make the most out of your Wood Pellet Smoker & Grill. The next step is to make some tasty foods and take pleasure in them! So, don't hesitate and grab your Wood Pellet Smoker & Grill with this cookbook before the opportunity passes you by.

Once you know the basics of pellet grilling, you see how easy it is to cook healthier foods. The only thing that's left to do is make sure you are doing a full service of your pellet grill. Cooking foods, while enjoyable to most folks, is what everyone likes to do. You already know about wood pellet grilling, and it's time to share your knowledge.

WOOD PELLET SMOKER COOKBOOK

50 DELICIOUS AND EASY RECIPES TO MASTER THE USE OF YOUR WOOD PELLET SMOKER AND GRILL

JORDAN WOOD

Introduction

The Wood Pellet Smoker-Grill utilizes wood pellets, which makes temperature and flavor control easier when smoking, grilling, or roasting. The ease of use has made this smoker-grill popular all around the globe.

Each Wood Pellet Smoker-Grill contains a storage hopper. This storage hopper is the place where you add all of the wood pellets. The equipment takes care of the transfer of wood pellets from the storage hopper to the burning area in the correct quantity.

Thus, you get a perfect temperature for the type of cooking approach you are following. The rate of pellet burning increases when you are grilling, and it decreases when you set the smoker-grill at a low temperature. This helps to smoke your food for a long time with a consistent heat.

It only takes about 10–20 minutes to heat and get the smoker-grill ready for cooking. The preheating process usually takes about 15 minutes. This makes cooking efficient and easy for everyone. You can pick any time and work on some delicious recipes.

Internal Design of the Wood Pellet Smoke and Grill

Modern designs of Wood Pellet Smoker-Grills contain electronic functionality. Advanced design allows smoker-grills to manage temperature control and pellets on its own. The wood pellets are transferred to the burning area according to the cooking setting you provide. The one push of a button, you can allow the smoker-grill to take care of the temperature consistency and the flavors of the food inside.

Cooking Options with the Wood Pellet Smoke and Grill

This smoker-grill brings a whole new level of versatility to your cooking. You get more than six ways to cook different kinds of foods. For example, you can bake fish fillets, grill meat, and smoke as well. All in all, the smoker-grill allows you to smoke and grill indirectly and directly along with baking and roasting. This versatile approach to cooking makes this smoker-grill suitable for a variety food options, including chicken, turkey, beef, lamb, pork, and seafood.

Use of Different Wood Pellets In the Wood Pellet Smoke and Grill

Different types of wood pellets, such as apple, cherry, hickory, mesquite, and others, are used to obtain specific flavors in foods. Each type of wood pellet is considered suitable for certain types of foods. Knowing this is critically important so that you can get the best flavors out of your cooking.

1. Apple wood pellets are generally used when the food's main ingredient is pork, chicken, or vegetables.

2. Cherry wood pellets are perfect for baking food, including pork, lamb, chicken, and beef.
3. Hickory wood pellets make pork, beef, vegetables, and even poultry exceptionally delicious.

Along with these three types, there are other wood pellet options, such as alder, maple, mesquite, pecan, and oak. Pork dishes can get the best flavors with almost all kinds of wood pellets except oak and mesquite. Oak, alder, and mesquite types are more effective when you want to cook fish, shrimp, or other kinds of seafood.

The Wood Pellet Smoke and Grill is a durable and cost-effective option for anyone who wants to smoke or grill without worrying all the time. Because of its quality of construction, it works effectively for a long time. You only need to spend a few minutes after cooking to maintain its cleanliness. This keeps the fuel efficiency high and allows for controlled wood pellet burning.

History of the Wood Pellet Smoke and Grill

The very first Wood Pellet Smoker-Grill was introduced in 1985. Joe Traeger was the man behind the concept and the construction of the Wood Pellet Smoker-Grill. After spending a year creating his smoker-grill, he obtained a patent and started production at a commercial level. The smoker-grill looked similar to traditional smokers in terms of its exterior design. There was a drum barrel and a chimney. But the internal components were the true magic. Traeger divided the internal design into three parts. These three parts were the sections where wood pellets had to go in order to get burned.

The storage hopper was the first part, which worked as storage for the wood pellets in the smoker-grill. Then, the next stop for the pellets was the auger, which was a rotating section. This rotation allowed wood pellets to reach the third and final section. This final section was called a firebox or burning box. In this area, a fan allowed the proper distribution of the cultivated heat.

In the early designs, the user had to light the smoker-grill manually. However, the design got updated with time, and now, there are completely automatic Wood Pellet Smoker-Grills available.

The reduction in wood pellet size revolutionized the whole smoking and grilling process. The machine obtained the ability to balance the temperatures on its own for as long as required. This convenience wasn't available with charcoal burning smokers. At the same time, wood pellets also provided more variety based on the flavorful hardwood choices available.

That would not be wrong to say that the BBQ world experienced a revolution with the introduction of the Wood Pellet Smoker-Grill. Cooking got simpler and more comfortable, which gave even newbies a chance to smoke, grill, bake, and roast. The machine was capable of handling the temperature on its own, so the users could be stress-free and safe when cooking. In 2007, after the expiration of Traeger's patent, the Wood Pellet Smoker-Grill market opened for more advanced options. This led to more advancements and automation in the equipment.

Beef

Garlic Butter Grilled Steak

Preparation Time: 15 minutes

Cooking Time: 25 minutes

Servings: 4

Ingredients:

- 3 tablespoons of unsalted butter
- 4 cloves of garlic
- 1 tablespoon of chopped parsley
- 1 tablespoon of olive oil
- 4 strip steaks

- Salt and pepper to taste

Directions:

Using a large mixing bowl, add in the butter, garlic, and parsley then mix properly to combine, set aside in the refrigerator.

Preheat a Wood Pellet Smoker and Grill to 400 degrees F, use paper towels to pat the steak dry, rub oil on all sides then season with some sprinkles of salt and pepper to taste.

Place the seasoned steak on the preheated grill and grill for about four to five minutes.

Flip the steak over and grill for an additional four to five minutes until it becomes brown in color and cooked as desired.

Rub the steak with the butter mixture, heat on the grill for a few minutes, slice, and serve.

Nutrition:

Calories: 543

Fat: 25g

Carbs: 1g

Protein: 64g

Beef Jerky

Preparation Time: 30 minutes

Cooking Time: 6 hours

Servings: 8

Ingredients:

- 1 cup pineapple juice
- ½ cup brown sugar
- 2 tablespoon sriracha
- 2 teaspoon onion powder
- 2 tablespoon minced garlic
- 2 tablespoon rice wine vinegar
- 2 tablespoon hoisin
- 1 teaspoon salt

- 1 tablespoon red pepper flakes
- 1 tablespoon coarsely ground black pepper
- 2 cups coconut aminos
- 2 jalapenos (thinly sliced)

Meat:

- 3 pounds trimmed sirloin steak (sliced to ¼ inch thick)

Directions:

Combine all the marinade ingredients in a mixing bowl and mix until the ingredients are well combined.

Put the sliced sirloin in a gallon sized zip-lock bag and pour the marinade into the bag. Massage the marinade into the beef. Seal the bag and refrigerate for 8 hours.

Remove the zip-lock bag from the refrigerator.

Activate the pellet grill smoker setting and leave lip opened for 5 minutes until fire starts.

Close the lid and preheat your pellet grill to 180°F, using hickory pellet.

Remove the beef slices from the marinade and pat them dry with a paper towel.

Arrange the beef slice on the grill in a single layer. Smoke the beef for about 4 to 5 hours, turning often after the first 2 hours of smoking. The jerky should be dark and dry when it is done.

Remove the jerky from the grill and let it sit for about 1 hour to cool.

Serve immediately or store in airtight container and refrigerate for future use.

Nutrition:

Carbohydrates: 12 g

Protein: 28 g

Fat: 16 g

Sodium: 23 mg

Cholesterol: 21 mg

Beef Skewers

Preparation Time: 30 minutes

Cooking Time: 5 hours

Servings: 8

Ingredients:

- 2 tablespoon olive oil
- 2 pounds top round steak (cut to ¼-inch-thick and 2-inch-wide slices)
- 2 garlic cloves (finely chopped)
- ¼ cup water

- ½ cup soy sauce
- ¾ cup brown sugar
- 1 tablespoon minced fresh ginger
- 1 teaspoon freshly ground black pepper or more to taste
- 3 tablespoon red wine vinegar
- 3 tablespoon dried basil
- Wooden or bamboo skewers (soaked in water for 30 minutes, at least)

Directions:

In a mixing bowl, combine the olive oil, sugar, ginger, garlic, soy sauce, water, vinegar, pepper and basil. Mix until the ingredients are well combined.

Pour the marinade into a zip-lock bag and add the steak slices. Massage the marinade into the steak slices. Refrigerate for 12 hours or more.

Remove the steak slices from the marinade and pat them dry with paper towel.

Thread the steak slices on to the soaked skewers.

Activate the smoke setting on your wood smoker grill, using a hickory wood pellet. Leave the lid opened until the fire is established.

Close the lid and preheat grill to 325°F for direct heat cooking.

Arrange the skewered steak unto the grill and grill 8 minutes or until the meat is done, turning occasionally.

Remove the skewered meat from the grill and let them sit for a few minutes to cool.

Serve warm and enjoy.

Nutrition:

Carbohydrates: 12 g

Protein: 28 g

Fat: 16 g

Sodium: 23 mg

Cholesterol: 21 mg

Grilled Coffee Rub Brisket

Preparation Time: 30 minutes

Cooking Time: 15 hours

Servings: 4

Ingredients:

- 1 (14 pounds) whole brisket
- Coffee Rub
- 2 tablespoons of coa rse salt to taste
- 2 tablespoons of instant coffee
- 2 tablespoons of garlic powder
- 2 tablespoons of smoked paprika
- 1 tablespoon of pepper to taste

- 1 tablespoon of crushed coriander
- 1 tablespoon of onion powder
- 1 teaspoon of chili powder
- 1/2 teaspoon of cayenne

Directions:

Using a large mixing bowl, add in the instant coffee, garlic powder, paprika, coriander, onion powder, chili powder, cayenne, salt, and pepper to taste then mix properly to combine.

Rub the brisket with the prepared rub, coating all sides then set aside.

Preheat a Wood Pellet Smoker and Grill to 225 degrees F, add in the seasoned brisket, cover the smoker, and smoke for about eight hours until a thermometer reads 165 degrees for the briskets.

Place the brisket in an aluminum foil then wrap up. Place the foil-wrapped brisket on the wood Pellet smoker and cook for another five to eight hours until the meat reaches an internal temperature of 225 degrees F.

Once cooked, let the brisket rest on the cutting board for about one hour, slice against the grain then serve.

Nutrition:

Calories: 420; Fat: 11g; Carbs: 15g

Grilled Herb Steak

Preparation Time: 15 minutes

Cooking Time: 20 minutes

Servings: 4

Ingredients:

- tablespoon of peppercorns
- 1 teaspoon of fennel seeds
- 3 large and minced cloves of garlic
- 2 teaspoons of kosher salt to taste
- 1 tablespoon of chopped rosemary
- 1 tablespoon of chopped thyme
- 2 teaspoons of black pepper to taste
- 2 teaspoons of olive oil
- 1 pound of flank steak

Directions:

Using a grinder or a food processor, add in the peppercorns and the fennel seeds then blend until completely crushed then add to a mixing bowl.

Add in the garlic, rosemary, thyme, salt, and pepper to taste then mix properly to combine, set aside.

Rub the steak with oil, coating all sides then coat with half of the peppercorn mixture. Make sure the steak is coated all round.

Place the steak in a Ziploc plastic bag then let marinate in the refrigerator for about 2 to 8 minutes.

Preheat a Wood Pellet Smoker and Grill to 450 degrees F, place the coated steak on the grill and cook for about five to six minutes.

Flip the steak over and cook for another five to six minutes until cooked through.

Once cooked, let the steak cool for a few minutes, slice, and serve.

Nutrition:

Calories: 440; Fat: 25g; Carbs: 20g; Protein: 35g

BBQ Meatloaf

Preparation Time: 25 minutes

Cooking Time: 1 hour and 30 minutes

Servings: 4

Ingredients:

- 1 1/2 pounds of ground beef
- 1/3 cup of ketchup
- 2 teaspoons of Worcestershire sauce
- 1 large egg
- 1 cup of soft breadcrumbs
- 1 cup of chopped onions
- 1/2 teaspoon of salt to taste

- 1/4 teaspoon of ground black pepper to taste
- Barbecue sauce for a glaze

Directions:

Preheat a Wood Pellet Smoker and Grill to 350 degrees F, using a large mixing bowl, add in the beef alongside with the rest of the ingredients on the list (aside from the barbecue sauce) them mix properly to combine.

Place the beef mixture in an aluminum foil then form into your desired loaf shape.

Unfold the foil, brush the meatloaf with barbecue sauce then warp in.

Place the meatloaf on the grill and cook for about 1 hour to 1 hour and 30 minutes until it attains a temperature of 160 degrees F.

Slice and serve.

Nutrition:

Calories: 370

Fat: 15g

Carbs: 20g

Protein: 35g

Wood Pellet Cocoa Rub Steak

Preparation Time: 20 minutes

Cooking Time: 40 minutes

Servings: 4

Ingredients:

- 4 ribeye steaks
- 2 tablespoons of unsweetened cocoa powder
- 1 tablespoon of dark brown sugar
- 1 tablespoon of smoked paprika
- 1 teaspoon of sea salt to taste
- 1 teaspoon of black pepper

- 1/2 teaspoon of garlic powder
- 1/2 teaspoon of onion powder

Directions:

Using a large mixing bowl, add in the cocoa powder, brown sugar, paprika, garlic powder, onion powder, and salt to taste then mix properly to combine

Rub the steak with about two tablespoons of the spice mixture, coating all sides then let rest for a few minutes.

Preheat the Wood Pellet Smoker and Grill to 450 degrees F, place the steak on the grill, and grill for a few minutes on both sides until it is cooked as desired.

Once cooked, cover the steak in a foil and let rest for a few minutes, serve and enjoy.

Nutrition:

Calories: 480

Fat: 30g

Carbs: 4g

Protein: 40g

Pork

Grilled Pork Chops

Preparation Time: 20 minutes

Cooking Time: 10 minutes

Servings: 6

Ingredients:

- 6 pork chops, thickly cut
- Bbq Rub

Directions:

Preheat the wood pellet to 450°F.

Season the pork chops generously with the BBQ rub. Place the pork chops on the grill and cook for 6 minutes or until the internal temperature reaches 145°F.

Remove from the grill and let sit for 10 minutes before serving.

Nutrition:

Calories 264

Total fat 13g

Saturated fat 6g

Total Carbs 4g

Net Carbs 1g

Protein 33g

Sugar 0g

Fiber 3g

Sodium: 66mg

Blackened Pork Chops

Preparation Time: 5 minutes

Cooking Time: 20 minutes

Servings: 6

Ingredients:

- 6 pork chops
- 1/4 cup blackening seasoning
- Salt and pepper to taste

Directions:

Preheat your grill to 375°F.

Meanwhile, generously season the pork chops with the blackening seasoning, salt, and pepper.

Place the pork chops on the grill and close the lid.

Let grill for 8 minutes then flip the chops. Cook until the internal temperature reaches 142°F.

Remove the chops from the grill and let rest for 10 minutes before slicing.

Serve and enjoy.

Nutrition:

Calories 333

Total fat 18g

Saturated fat 6g

Total Carbs 1g

Net Carbs 0g

Protein 40g

Sodium: 3175mg

Grilled Tenderloin with Fresh Herb Sauce

Preparation Time: 10 minutes

Cooking Time: 15 minutes

Servings: 4

Ingredients:

- 1 pork tenderloin, silver skin removed and dried
- BBQ seasoning
- 1 handful basil, fresh

- 1/4 tbsp. garlic powder
- 1/3 cup olive oil
- 1/2 tbsp. kosher salt

Directions:

Preheat the wood pellet grill to medium heat.

Coat the pork with BBQ seasoning then cook on semi-direct heat of the grill. Turn the pork regularly to ensure even cooking.

Cook until the internal temperature is 145°F. Remove from the grill and leave it for 10 minutes.

Meanwhile, make the herb sauce by pulsing all the sauce ingredients in a food processor. Pulse for a few times or until well chopped.

Slice the pork diagonally and spoon the sauce on top. Serve and enjoy.

Nutrition:

Calories 300

Total fat 22g

Total Carbs 13g

Net Carbs 12g

Protein 14g

Pork Tenderloin

Preparation Time: 7 minutes

Cooking Time: 90 minutes

Servings: 5

Ingredients:

- 1 Pork tenderloin GMG Pork Rub
- 1 Cup of Teriyaki Sauce

Directions:

You can use 1 to two pork tenderloins. Generously rub the pork tenderloins with the Green Mountain Pork Rub and let it stand aside for about 4 to 24 hours.

Set your Smoker grill at 320°F (160°C) and when the grill reaches the Smoke Temperature you are looking for, place in the tenderloin and baste both the sides with a sweet marinade like the Teriyaki sauce

Cook for about 1 and ¼ hours while turning frequently or just until the internal Smoke Temperature displays at least 165° F.

Be careful not to overcook the tenderloin because it may lead to obtaining a dry meat.

Serve and enjoy your dish!

Nutrition:

Calories: 125

Fat: 29g

Carbohydrates: 3.5g

Protein: 22 g

Apple Orange Pork Loin Roast

Preparation Time: 5 minutes

Cooking Time: about 42 minutes

Servings: 6

Ingredients:

- Peppercorns—6
- Pork loin—1 5lb.
- roast Orange juice—½ cup
- Lemon—1, halved
- Kosher salt—½ cup
- Ice water—1 cup

- Fennel seeds—½ tsp.
- Brown sugar—¼ cup
- Olive oil—2 tbsps.
- Pepper flakes—½ tsp.
- Garlic—3 cloves
- Pepper and salt—as required
- Apple juice—½ cup
- Bay leaves 2
- For the sauce:
- Cognac—1 cup
- Butter—2 tbsps.
- Pepper flakes—½ tsp.
- Sugar—1 cup
- Minced garlic—½ tsp.
- Apple juice—½ cup
- Lemon—1, halved
- Shallot—1, sliced thinly
- Orange juice—½ cup
- Fennel seeds—½ tsp.
- Fresh figs—1 pint, quartered
- Ice water—1 cup

Directions:

In a large enough pot, prepare a mixture of brown sugar, salt, bay leaves, garlic, lemon, peppercorns, pepper flakes, fennel seeds, orange juice, and apple. Heat and simmer to dissolve sugar and salt.

Transfer the mixture to a container with ice water and refrigerate.

In the cooled brine, add pork roast and submerge. Refrigerate for 8–12 hours.

Take out the roast, rinse it, and use paper towels to pat dry.

Use olive oil to coat the roast and season with pepper and salt.

Prepare your Smoker-Grill by preheating it to a high Smoke Temperature as per factory method Close the top lid and leave for 12–18 minutes.

Roast the meat on the grilling grate for about 23–26 minutes until the internal Smoke Temperature reaches 140°F.

Remove and allow the meat to cool before slicing.

Combine all ingredients for the sauce and heat in butter in a large enough pan. Simmer for about 20–30 minutes to reach desired thickness. Pour the sauce over the sliced pork roast. Your dish is ready to be served.

Nutrition:

Carbohydrate—18 g

Protein—72 g

Fat—22 g

Sodium—567 mg

Pork Bone-In Chops with Rosemary and Thyme

Preparation Time: 8 minutes

Cooking Time: about 52 minutes

Servings: 6

Ingredients:

- Butter—2 tbsps.
- Pork—4 chops, bone-in
- Rosemary—1 sprig
- Thyme—2 sprigs

- Pork rubs—according to taste

Directions:

Prepare your Smoker-Grill by preheating it to a Smoke Temperature of about 180°F. Close the top lid and leave for 12–18 minutes.

Use pork rub to properly coat the chops.

Transfer to the grilling grate and let the chops smoke for about 35–40 minutes. This should bring the internal Smoke Temperature to 130°F.

Remove and set aside the chops so they can cool down.

Increase the Smoke Temperature of the smoker-grill to high and let the grilling grate preheat.

In a cast iron pan, combine the herbs, butter, and pork chops.

Sear the chops, 3–5 minutes on each side.

Remove and let the chops cool for about 8–10 minutes.

Your dish is ready to be served.

Nutrition:

Carbohydrate—22 g; Protein—23 g; Fat—15 g

Smoked Pork Ribs Black Pepper

Preparation Time: 30 minutes

Cooking Time: 6hours

Servings: 1

Ingredients:

- Pork Baby Back Ribs (6-lbs., 2.7-kgs)
- Salt – ½ cup
- Black pepper – ¾ c up
- Sweet smoked paprika – 1 tablespoon
- Sugar – 3 tablespoons

- Mustard powder – 1 tablespoon

The Fire

Preheat the smoker an hour prior to smoking.

Use charcoal and peach wood chips for smoking.

Directions:

Combine salt with black pepper, sweet smoked paprika, sugar, and mustard powder. Stir until mixed.

Rub the pork baby ribs with the salt mixture then place in disposable aluminum pan. Set aside.

Preheat the smoker to 225°F (107°C) with charcoal and peach wood chips then wait until it reaches the desired temperature.

Once the smoker is ready, place the disposable aluminum pan in the smoker.

Smoke the pork baby ribs for 6 hours or until the internal temperature has reached 205°F (96°C).

Remove the smoked pork ribs from the smoker then transfer to a serving dish.

Serve and enjoy.

Nutrition:

Carbohydrates: 4g

Protein: 86 g

Fat: 46 g

Sodium: 181 mg

Cholesterol: 295 mg

Pork Collar and Rosemary Marinade

Preparation Time: 15 minutes

Cooking Time: 30 minutes

Servings: 4

Ingredients:

- 1 pork collar, 3-4 pounds
- 3 tablespoons rosemary, fresh
- 3 shallots, minced
- 2 tablespoons garlic, chopped
- ½ cup bourbon

- 2 teaspoons coriander, ground
- 1 bottle of apple ale
- 1 teaspoon ground black pepper
- 2 teaspoons salt
- 3 tablespoons oil

Directions:

Take a zip bag and add pepper, salt, canola oil, apple ale, bourbon, coriander, garlic, shallots, and rosemary and mix well

Cut meat into slabs and add them to the marinade, let it refrigerate overnight

Pre-heat your smoker to 450 degrees F

Transfer meat to smoker and smoke for 5 minutes, lower Smoke Temperature to 325 degrees F

Pour marinade all over and cook for 25 minutes more until the internal Smoke Temperature reaches 160 degrees F

Serve and enjoy!

Nutrition:

Calories: 420; Fats: 26g; Carbs: 4g

Roasted Ham

Preparation Time: 15 minutes

Cooking Time: 2 hours 15 minutes

Servings: 4

Ingredients:

- 8-10 pounds ham, bone-in
- 2 tablespoons mustard, Dijon

- ¼ cup horseradish
- 1 bottle BBQ Apricot Sauce

Directions:

Pre-heat your smoker to 325 degrees F

Cover a roasting pan with foil and place the ham, transfer to smoker and smoke for 1 hour and 30 minutes

Take a small pan and add sauce, mustard, and horseradish, place it over medium heat and cook for a few minutes

Keep it on the side

After 1 hour 30 minutes of smoking, glaze ham and smoke for 30 minutes more until the internal Smoke Temperature reaches 135 degrees F

Let it rest for 20 minutes, slice and enjoy!

Nutrition:

Calories: 460

Fats: 43g

Carbs: 10g

Lamb

Stuffed Leg of Lamb

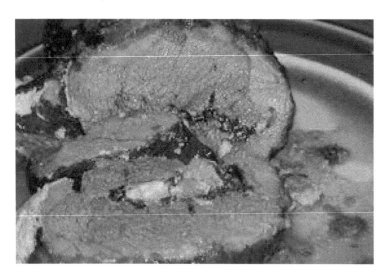

Preparation Time: 20 minutes

Cooking Time: 2½ hours

Servings: 8

Ingredients:

- 1 (8-ounce) package cream cheese, softened
- ¼ cup cooked bacon, crumbled
- 1 jalapeño pepper, seeded and chopped
- 1 tablespoon dried rosemary, crushed
- 2 teaspoons garlic powder

- 1 teaspoon onion powder
- 1 teaspoon paprika
- 1 teaspoon cayenne pepper
- Salt, as required
- 1 (4-5-pound) leg of lamb, butterflied
- 2-3 tablespoons olive oil

Directions:

Preheat the Z Grills Wood Pellet Grill & Smoker on smoke setting to 225-240 degrees F, using charcoal and cherry wood chips.

For filling: in a bowl, add all ingredients and mix until well combined.

For spice mixture: in another small bowl, mix together all ingredients.

Place the leg of lamb onto a smooth surface.

Sprinkle the inside of leg with some spice mixture.

Place filling mixture over the inside surface evenly.

Roll the leg of lamb tightly and with a butcher's twine, tie the roll to secure the filling

Coat the outer side of roll with olive oil evenly and then sprinkle with spice mixture.

Arrange the leg of lamb onto the grill and cook for about 2-2½ hours.

Remove the leg of lamb from grill and place onto a cutting board.

With a piece of foil cover the leg of lamb loosely for about 20-25 minutes before serving.

 With a sharp knife, cut the leg of lamb into desired-sized slices and serve.

Nutrition:

Calories 700

Total Fat 37.2 g

Saturated Fat 15.2 g

Cholesterol 294 mg

Sodium 478 mg

Total Carbs 2.2 g

Fiber 0.5 g

Sugar 0.5 g

Protein 84.6 g

Seasoned Lamb Shoulder

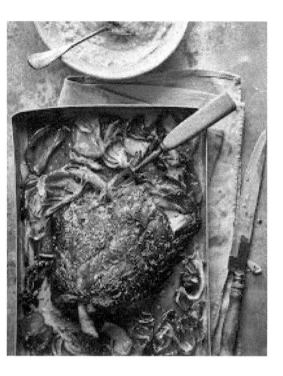

Preparation Time: 15 minutes

Cooking Time: 5¾ hours

Servings: 6

Ingredients:

- 1 (5-pound) bone-in lamb shoulder, trimmed
- 3-4 tablespoons Moroccan seasoning
- 2 tablespoons olive oil
- 1 cup water

- ¼ cup apple cider vinegar

Directions:

Preheat the Z Grills Wood Pellet Grill & Smoker on smoke setting to 275 degrees F, using charcoal.

Coat the lamb shoulder with oil evenly and then rub with Moroccan seasoning generously.

Place the lamb shoulder onto the grill and cook for about 45 minutes.

In a food-safe spray bottle, mix together vinegar and water.

Spray the lamb shoulder with vinegar mixture evenly.

Cook for about 4-5 hours, spraying with vinegar mixture after every 20 minutes.

Remove the lamb shoulder from grill and place onto a cutting board for about 20 minutes before slicing.

With a sharp knife, cut the lamb shoulder in desired sized slices and serve.

Nutrition:

Calories 563; Total Fat 25.2 g; Total Carbs 3.1 g; Protein 77.4 g

Lemony & Spicy Lamb Shoulder

Preparation Time: 15 minutes

Cooking Time: 2½ hours

Servings: 8

Ingredients:

- 1 (5-pound) bone-in lamb shoulder, trimmed
- 2 tablespoons olive oil
- 1 tablespoon fresh lemon juice
- 1 tablespoon fresh ginger, peeled

- 4-6 garlic cloves, peeled
- ½ tablespoon ground cumin
- ½ tablespoon paprika
- ½ tablespoon ground turmeric
- ½ tablespoon ground allspice
- Salt and ground black pepper, as required

Directions:

Using a sharp knife, carve the skin of the lamb shoulder into diamond pattern.

Combine all the ingredients in a food processor and pulse until smooth.

Coat the lamb shoulder with pureed mixture generously.

Arrange the lamb shoulder into a large baking dish and refrigerate, covered overnight.

Remove the baking dish of shoulder from refrigerator and set aside at room temperature for at least 1 hour before cooking.

Preheat the Z Grills Wood Pellet Grill & Smoker on grill setting to 225 degrees F.

Place the lamb shoulder onto the grill and cook for about 2½ hours.

Remove the lamb shoulder from grill and place onto a cutting board for about 20 minutes before slicing.

With a sharp knife, cut the lamb shoulder into desired-sized slices and serve.

Nutrition:

Calories 417

Total Fat 18.8 g

Saturated Fat 5.6 g

Cholesterol 188 mg

Sodium 222 mg

Total Carbs 2 g

Fiber 0.5 g

Sugar 0.1 g

Protein 58.1 g

Sweet & Tangy Braised Lamb Shank

Preparation Time: 15 minutes

Cooking Time: 10 hours

Servings: 2

Ingredients:

- 2 (1¼-pound) lamb shanks
- 1-2 cups water
- ¼ cup brown sugar
- 1/3 cup rice wine
- 1/3 cup soy sauce
- 1 tablespoon dark sesame oil
- 4 (1½x½-inch) orange zest strips

- 2 (3-inch long) cinnamon sticks
- 1½ teaspoons Chinese five spice powder

Directions:

Preheat the Z Grills Wood Pellet Grill & Smoker on smoke setting to 225-250 degrees F, using charcoal and soaked apple wood chips.

With a sharp knife, pierce each lamb shank at many places.

In a bowl, add remaining all ingredients and mix until sugar is dissolved.

In a large foil pan, place the lamb shanks and top with sugar mixture evenly.

Place the foil pan onto the grill and cook for about 8-10 hours, flipping after every 30 minutes. (If required, add enough water to keep the liquid ½-inch over).

Remove from the grill and serve hot.

Nutrition:

Calories 1200; Total Fat 48.4 g; Saturated Fat 15.8 g; Total Carbs 39.7 g; Sugar 29 g; Protein 161.9 g

Cheesy Lamb Burgers

Preparation Time: 10 minutes

Cooking Time: 18 minutes

Servings: 4

Ingredients:

- 2 pounds ground lamb
- 1 cup Parmigiano-Reggiano cheese, grated
- Salt and ground black pepper, as required

Directions:

Preheat the Z Grills Wood Pellet Grill & Smoker on grill setting to 425 degrees F.

In a bowl, add all ingredients and mix until well combined.

Make 4 (¾-inch thick) patties from mixture.

With your thumbs, make a shallow but wide depression in each patty.

Arrange the patties onto the grill, depression-side down and cook for about 8 minutes.

Flip the patties and cook for about 8-10 minutes.

Remove the patties from grill and serve immediately.

Nutrition:

Calories 502

Total Fat 22.6 g

Saturated Fat 9.9 g

Cholesterol 220 mg

Sodium 331 mg

Total Carbs 0 g

Protein 71.7 g

Poultry

Barbecue Chicken Breasts

Preparation Time: 20 minutes

Cooking Time: 30 minutes

Servings: 4

Ingredients:

- Two T. Worcestershire sauce
- ½ c. hot barbecue sauce
- One c. barbecue sauce

- Two cloves minced garlic
- ¼ c. olive oil
- 4 chicken breasts

Directions:

Put the chicken breasts into a deep container.

In another bowl, put the Worcestershire sauce, barbecue sauces, garlic, and olive oil. Stir well to combine.

Use half to marinate the chicken and reserve the rest for basting.

Add wood pellets to your smoker and follow your cooker's startup procedure. Preheat your smoker, with your lid closed, until it reaches 350.

Take the chicken breasts out of the sauce. On the grill, place them before smoking them for approximately 20 minutes.

About ten minutes before the chicken is finished, baste with reserved barbecue sauce.

Nutrition:

Calories: 220; Protein: 27g; Carbs: 19g; Fat: 3.3g

Cilantro-Lime Chicken

Preparation Time: 50 minutes

Cooking Time: 5 hours

Servings: 4

Ingredients:

- Pepper
- Salt
- 4 cloves minced garl ic
- ½ c. lime juice
- One c. honey
- Two T. olive oil
- ½ c. chopped cilantro

- 4 chicken breasts

Directions:

Put the chicken breasts into a large zip-top bag.

In another bowl, put the pepper, salt, olive oil, garlic, honey, lime juice, and cilantro. Stir well to combine.

Use half as a marinade and reserve the rest for later.

Place into the refrigerator for four to five hours.

Add wood pellets to your smoker and follow your cooker's startup procedure. Preheat your smoker, with your lid closed, until it reaches 350.

Remove the chicken breasts the bag. Use paper towels to pat them dry. Let them smoke up in the grill for about fifteen minutes

Baste with reserved marinade.

Nutrition:

Calories: 62.5

Protein: 8.2g

Carbs: 3g

Fat: 2g

Lemon Honey Chicken

Preparation Time: 30 minutes

Cooking Time: 30 minutes

Servings: 4

Ingredients:

- Pepper
- Salt
- Chopped rosemary
- One clove crushed garlic
- One T. honey
- Juice of one lemon

- ½ c. chicken broth
- 3 T. butter
- 4 chicken breasts

Directions:

Put a pan over the stove and melt the butter. Place chicken breasts into hot butter and sear on each side until a nice color has formed.

Take out of the pan and allow to rest for ten minutes.

In a small bowl, put the pepper, salt, rosemary, garlic, honey, lemon juice, and broth. Stir well to combine.

Rub each breast with the honey lemon mixture.

Add wood pellets to your smoker and follow your cooker's startup procedure. Preheat your smoker, with your lid closed, until it reaches 350.

Put the chicken breasts onto the preheated grill and grill for 20 minutes.

Nutrition:

Calories: 265.1

Protein: 31.1g

Carbs: 25.3g

Fat: 7g

Mediterranean Chicken

Preparation Time: 30 minutes

Cooking Time: 3 hours

Servings: 6

Ingredients:

- Lemon slices to garnish
- Salt
- Pepper
- One t. chopped rosemary
- 3 cloves minced garlic
- Zest of one lemon
- One t. oregano
- Small chopped onion
- ½ c. white wine

- ¼ c. olive oil
- 4 chicken breasts

Directions:

Put the chicken breasts into a large zip-top bag.

In another bowl, put the olive oil, white wine, lemon zest, onion, garlic, oregano, rosemary, pepper, and salt. Stir well to combine.

Coat the chicken in this mixture. Place into the refrigerator for two to three hours.

Add wood pellets to your smoker and follow your cooker's startup procedure. Preheat your smoker, with your lid closed, until it reaches 350.

The chicken breast should be removed from the bag before patting them dry with paper towels. Place them on the grill and smoke for 15 minutes.

Leave it for 10 minutes before slicing. Garnish with sliced lemon.

Nutrition:

Calories: 330.6; Protein: 57.3g; Carbs: 15.1g; Fat: 3.6g

Smoked Whole Duck

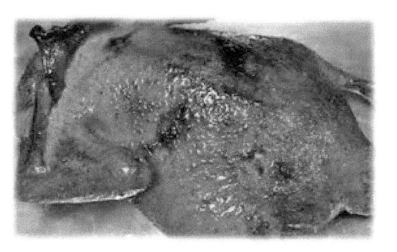

Preparation Time: 15 minutes

Cooking Time: 2 hours 30 minutes

Servings: 6

Ingredients:

- 5 pounds whole duck (trimmed of any excess fat)
- 1 small onion (quartered)
- 1 apple (wedged)
- 1 orange (quartered)
- 1 tbsp freshly chopped parsley
- 1 tbsp freshly chopped sage
- ½ tsp onion powder

- 2 tsp smoked paprika
- 1 tsp dried Italian seasoning
- 1 tbsp dried Greek seasoning
- 1 tsp pepper or to taste
- 1 tsp sea salt or to taste

Directions:

Remove giblets and rinse duck, inside and pour, under cold running water.

Pat dry with paper towels.

Use the tip of a sharp knife to cut the duck skin all over. Be careful not to cut through the meat. Tie the duck legs together with butcher's string.

To make a rub, combine the onion powder, pepper, salt, Italian seasoning, Greek seasoning, and paprika in a mixing bowl.

Insert the orange, onion, and apple to the duck cavity. Stuff the duck with freshly chopped parsley and sage.

Season all sides of the duck generously with rub mixture.

Start your pellet grill on smoke mode, leaving the lip open or until the fire starts.

Close the lid and preheat the grill to 325°F for 10 minutes.

Place the duck on the grill grate.

Roast for 2 to 21/2 hours, or until the duck skin is brown and the internal temperature of the thigh reaches 160°F.

Remove the duck from heat and let it rest for a few minutes.

Cut into sizes and serve.

Nutrition:

Calories: 809

Total Fat:: 42.9 g

Saturated Fat: 15.8 g

Cholesterol: 337 mg

Sodium: 638 mg

Total Carbohydrate: 11.7 g

Dietary Fiber: 2.4 g

Total Sugars: 7.5 g

Protein: 89.6 g

Sweet and Sour Chicken Drumsticks

Preparation Time: 30 minutes

Cooking Time: 2hours

Servings: 1

Ingredients:

- 8 pieces of chicken drumsticks
- 2 tablespoon of rice wine vinegar
- 3 tablespoon brown sugar
- 1 cup of ketchup
- ¼ cup of soy sauce

- Minced garlic
- 2 tablespoons of honey
- 1 tablespoon of sweet heat rub
- Minced ginger
- ½ lemon; juice
- 1/2 juiced lime

Directions:

Take a mixing bowl and add soy sauce along with brown sugar, ketchup, lemon, rice wine vinegar, sweet heat rub, honey, ginger, and garlic.

Now keep half of the mixture for dipping sauce and therefore set it aside

Take the leftover half and pour it in a plastic bag that can be re-sealed

Now add drumsticks to it and then seal the bag again

Refrigerate it for 4 to 12 hours

Take out the chicken from the bag and discard the marinade

Fire the grill and set the temperature to 225 degrees F

Now smoke the chicken over indirect heat for 2 to 3 hours a make sure to turn it once or twice

Add more glaze if needed

Remove it from the grill and let it stand aside for 10 minutes

Add more sauce or keep it as a dipping sauce

Serve and enjoy

Nutrition:

Carbohydrates: 29 g

Protein: 19 g

Sodium: 25 mg

Cholesterol: 19 mg

Seafood

Simple Grilled Oysters

Preparation Time: 10 minutes

Cooking Time: 5 minutes

Servings: 8

Ingredients:

- 4 dozen oysters, scrubbed
- Lemon wedges
- 1 C butter
- 1 Tsp seasoned salt
- 1 tsp lemon pepper

Directions:

Preheat pellet grill to 350F.

Melt butter with seasoned salt and lemon pepper, mixing well. Simmer 10 minutes.

Place oysters, unshelled, on pellet grill.

Oysters have a "cup" side (like a bowl) and a "lid" side (flat), the cup side should be down so as not to lose all the yummy juices.

When shells pop open (3-5 minutes), use an oyster knife to detach oyster from top shell, and plop it back into the cup with the hot oyster liquor. Discard the lid.

Add a teaspoon of seasoned butter and serve.

Oysters that do not open should be discarded.

Nutrition:

Total Fat 26g

Saturated Fat 8g

Cholesterol 48mg

Protein 3g

Carbs 2g

Garlic Asiago Oysters

Preparation Time: 10 minutes

Cooking Time: 5 minutes

Servings: 12

Ingredients:

- 1 lb. sweet cream butter
- 1 Tbsp. minced garlic
- 2 dozen fresh oysters
- ½ C. grated Asiago cheese
- French bread, warmed
- ¼ cup chives, diced

Directions:

Start pellet grill and heat to medium high.

Melt butter over medium-high heat. Reduce heat to low and stir in garlic.

Cook 1 minute and remove from heat.

Place oysters, cup down, on pellet grill. As soon as shells pop open, remove from grill.

Shuck oysters, keeping as much of the oyster liquor in place as possible.

Cut connective muscle and return each oyster to its shell.

Drizzle each oyster with 2 teaspoons butter mixture and sprinkle with 1 teaspoon cheese. Grill over high heat 3 minutes or until cheese browns. Sprinkle with chives.

Remove from pellet grill and serve immediately with bread and remaining butter on the side.

Nutrition:

Calories: 681kcal

Carbohydrates: 68g

Protein: 23g

Fat: 35g

Saturated Fat: 20g

Cholesterol: 221mg

Sodium: 778mg

Potassium: 325mg

Fiber: 5g

Wasabi Oysters

Preparation Time: 20 minutes

Cooking Time: 5 minutes

Servings: 6

Ingredients:

- 12 small Pacific oysters, raw in shell 2 Tbsp. white wine vinegar
- 8 oz white wine 1/4 C shallots, minced
- 2 Tbsp. wasabi mustard 1 Tbsp. soy sauce
- 1 C unsalted butter, cubed 1 C chopped cilantro leaves
- Salt and black pepper to taste

Directions:

In a saucepan, over medium heat, combine the white wine vinegar, wine, and shallots. Simmer until the liquid is slightly reduced. Strain out shallots and discard, return liquid to the pan. Reduce heat to low. Add wasabi mustard and soy sauce, stirring.

Over low heat gradually whisks in butter. Do not let the mixture boil. When all the butter has been incorporated, stir in cilantro, and remove from heat. Pour into a small bowl and set aside.

Prepare a dish of coarse salt to hold the oyster shells in place.

Clean oysters thoroughly. Place oysters, flat side up, on the pellet grill preheated to medium, and close the lid. Cook oysters until shells just open (5-6 minutes). Remove oysters from the pellet grill and cut the connective muscle from the top shell, (careful – do not spill the liquor.) Turn the oyster over and return it to the cup half of shell. Discard the lid.

Press each oyster (in shell) into the coarse salt to keep it upright, then spoon 1-2 teaspoons of wasabi-butter sauce over each and serve immediately.

Be Prepared to cook a lot of oysters!

Nutrition:

Energy 208kj

Fat Total 8g

Saturated Fat 1g

Protein 19g

Carbohydrate 12g

Sugar 0g

Sodium 214mg

Crab Legs on the Grill

Preparation Time: 15 minutes

Cooking Time: 30 minutes

Servings: 4 - 6

Ingredients:

- 1 cup melted Butter
- 3 lb. Halved Crab Legs
- 2 tablespoon Lemon juice, fresh
- 1 tablespoon Old Bay
- 2 Garlic cloves, minced
- For garnish, chopped parsley
- For serving: Lemon wedges

Directions:

Place the crab legs in a roasting pan.

In a bowl combine the lemon juice, butter, and garlic. Mix. Pour over the legs. Coat well. Sprinkle with old bay.

Preheat the grill to 350F with closed lid.

Place the roasting pan on the grill and cook 20 - 30 minutes busting two times with the sauce in the pan.

Place the legs on a plate. Divide the crab sauce among 4 bowls for dipping.

Nutrition:

Calories: 170

Proteins: 20g

Carbohydrates: 0

Fiber: 0g

Fat: 8g

Seared Tuna Steaks

Preparation Time: 5 minutes

Cooking Time: 5 minutes

Servings: 2 - 4

Ingredients:

- 3 -inch Tuna
- Black pepper
- Sea Salt
- Olive oil
- Sriracha
- Soy Sauce

Directions:

Baste the tuna steaks with oil and sprinkle with black pepper and salt.

Preheat the grill to high with closed lid.

Grill the tuna for 2 ½ minutes per side.

Remove from the grill. Let it rest for 5 minutes.

Cut into thin pieces and serve with Sriracha and Soy Sauce. Enjoy.

Nutrition:

Calories: 120

Proteins: 34g

Carbohydrates: 0g

Fiber: 0g

Fat: 1.5g

Roasted Shrimp Mix

Preparation Time: 30 minutes

Cooking Time: 1h 30 minutes

Servings: 8 - 12

Ingredients:

- 3 lb. Shrimp (large), with tails, divided
- 2 lb. Kielbasa Smoked Sausage
- 6 corns cut into 3 pieces
- 2 lb. Potatoes, red
- Old Bay

Directions:

Preheat the grill to 275F with closed lid.

First, cook the sausage on the grill. Cook for 1 hour.

Increase the temperature to high. Season the corn and potatoes with Old Bay. Now roast until they become tender.

Season the shrimp with the Old Bay and cook on the grill for 20 minutes.

In a bowl combine the cooked ingredients. Toss.

Adjust seasoning with Old Bay and serve. Enjoy!

Nutrition:

Calories: 530

Proteins: 20g

Carbohydrates: 32g

Fat: 35g

Fiber: 1g

234

Vegetables

Roasted Parmesan Cheese Broccoli

Preparation Time: 5 minutes

Cooking Time: 45 minutes

Servings: 3 to 4

Ingredients:

- 3 cups broccoli, stems trimmed
- 1 tbsp lemon juice
- 1 tbsp olive oil
- 2 garlic cloves, minced
- 1/2 tsp kosher salt
- 1/2 tsp ground black pepper
- 1 tsp lemon zest
- 1/8 cup parmesan cheese, grated

Directions:

Preheat pellet grill to 375°F.

Place broccoli in a resealable bag. Add lemon juice, olive oil, garlic cloves, salt, and pepper. Seal the bag and toss to combine. Let the mixture marinate for 30 minutes.

Pour broccoli into a grill basket. Place basket on grill grates to roast. Grill broccoli for 14-18 minutes, flipping broccoli halfway through. Grill until tender yet a little crispy on the outside.

Remove broccoli from grill and place on a serving dish—zest with lemon and top with grated parmesan cheese. Serve immediately and enjoy!

Nutrition:

Calories: 82.6

Fat: 4.6 g

Cholesterol: 1.8 mg

Carbohydrate: 8.1 g

Fiber: 4.6 g

Sugar: 0

Protein: 5.5

Cajun Style Grilled Corn

Preparation Time: 5 minutes

Cooking Time: 25 minutes

Servings: 4

Ingredients:

- 4 ears corn, with husks
- 1 tsp dried oregano
- 1 tsp paprika
- 1 tsp garlic powder
- 1 tsp onion powder
- 1/2 tsp kosher salt
- 1/2 tsp ground black pepper
- 1/4 tsp dried thyme
- 1/4 tsp cayenne pepper
- 2 tsp butter, melted

Directions:

Preheat pellet grill to 375°F.

Peel husks back but do not remove. Scrub and remove silks.

Mix oregano, paprika, garlic powder, onion powder, salt, pepper, thyme, and cayenne in a small bowl.

Brush melted butter over corn.

Rub seasoning mixture over each ear of corn. Pull husks up and place corn on grill grates. Grill for about 12-15 minutes, turning occasionally.

Remove from grill and allow to cool for about 5 minutes. Remove husks, then serve and enjoy!

Nutrition:

Calories: 278

Fat: 17.4 g

Cholesterol: 40.7 mg

Carbohydrate: 30.6 g

Fiber: 4.5 g

Sugar: 4.6 g

Protein: 5.4 g

Smoked Healthy Cabbage

Preparation Time: 10 minutes

Cooking Time: 2 hours

Servings: 5

Ingredients:

- 1 head cabbage, cored
- 4 tablespoons butter
- 2 tablespoons rendered bacon fat
- 1 chicken bouillon cube
- 1 teaspoon fresh ground black pepper
- 1 garlic clove, minced

Directions:

Preheat your smoker to 240 degrees Fahrenheit using your preferred wood

Fill the hole of your cored cabbage with butter, bouillon cube, bacon fat, pepper and garlic

Wrap the cabbage in foil about two-thirds of the way up

Make sure to leave the top open

Transfer to your smoker rack and smoke for 2 hours

Unwrap and enjoy!

Nutrition:

Calories: 231

Fats: 10g

Carbs: 26g

Fiber: 1g

Grilled Cherry Tomato Skewers

Preparation Time: 10 minutes

Cooking Time: 50 minutes

Servings: 4

Ingredients:

- 24 cherry tomatoes
- 1/4 cup olive oil
- 3 tbsp balsamic vinegar
- 4 garlic cloves, minced
- 1 tbsp fresh thyme, finely chopped
- 1 tsp kosher salt
- 1 tsp ground black pepper
- 2 tbsp chives, finely chopped

Directions:

Preheat pellet grill to 425°F.

In a medium-sized bowl, mix olive oil, balsamic vinegar, garlic, and thyme. Add tomatoes and toss to coat.

Let tomatoes sit in the marinade at room temperature for about 30 minutes.

Remove tomatoes from marinade and thread 4 tomatoes per skewer.

Season both sides of each skewer with kosher salt and ground pepper.

Place on grill grate and grill for about 3 minutes on each side, or until each side is slightly charred.

Remove from grill and allow to rest for about 5 minutes. Garnish with chives, then serve and enjoy!

Nutrition:

Calories: 228

Fat: 10 g

Cholesterol: 70 mg

Carbohydrate: 7 g

Fiber: 2 g

Sugar: 3 g

Protein: 27 g

Roasted Vegetable Medley

Preparation Time: 20 minutes

Cooking Time: 50 minutes

Servings: 4 to 6

Ingredients:

- 2 medium potatoes, cut to 1 inch wedges
- 2 red bell peppers, cut into 1 inch cubes
- 1 small butternut squash, peeled and cubed to 1 inch cube
- red onion, cut to 1 inch cubes
- 1 cup broccoli, trimmed
- tbsp olive oil
- 1 tbsp balsamic vinegar
- 1 tbsp fresh rosemary, minced
- 1 tbsp fresh thyme, minced
- 1 tsp kosher salt
- 1 tsp ground black pepper

Directions:

Preheat pellet grill to 425°F.

In a large bowl, combine potatoes, peppers, squash, and onion.

In a small bowl, whisk together olive oil, balsamic vinegar, rosemary, thyme, salt, and pepper.

Pour marinade over vegetables and toss to coat. Allow resting for about 15 minutes.

Place marinated vegetables into a grill basket, and place a grill basket on the grill grate. Cook for about 30-40 minutes, occasionally tossing in the grill basket.

Remove veggies from grill and transfer to a serving dish. Allow to cool for 5 minutes, then serve and enjoy!

Nutrition:

Calories: 158.6

Fat: 7.4 g

Cholesterol: 0

Carbohydrate: 22 g

Fiber: 7.2 g

Sugar: 3.1 g

Protein: 5.2 g

Twice-Smoked Potatoes

Preparation Time: 10 minutes

Cooking Time: 14 minutes

Servings: 4

Ingredients:

- 8 Idaho, Russet, or Yukon Gold potatoes
- 1 (12-ounce) can evaporated milk, heated
- 1 cup (2 sticks) butter, melted
- ½ cup sour cream, at room temperature
- 1 cup grated Parmesan cheese
- ½ pound bacon, cooked and crumbled
- ¼ cup chopped scallions
- Salt
- Freshly ground black pepper
- 1 cup shredded Cheddar cheese

Directions:

Supply your smoker with wood pellets and follow the manufacturer's specific start-up procedure. Preheat, with the lid closed, to 400°F.

Poke the potatoes all over with a fork. Arrange them directly on the grill grate, close the lid, and smoke for 1 hour and 15 minutes, or until cooked through and they have some give when pinched.

Let the potatoes cool for 10 minutes, then cut in half lengthwise.

Into a medium bowl, scoop out the potato flesh, leaving ¼ inch in the shells; place the shells on a baking sheet.

Using an electric mixer on medium speed, beat the potatoes, milk, butter, and sour cream until smooth.

Stir in the Parmesan cheese, bacon, and scallions, and season with salt and pepper.

Generously stuff each shell with the potato mixture and top with Cheddar cheese.

Place the baking sheet on the grill grate, close the lid, and smoke for 20 minutes, or until the cheese is melted.

Technique Tip One extra step can give your potato a salty crust. Before baking, cover the raw potato with your choice of oil, bacon grease (YAASS!), or butter, then coat the spud with sea salt.

Nutrition:

Calories: 150

Carbohydrates: 15 g

Protein: 79 g

Sodium: 45 mg

Cholesterol: 49 mg

Desserts

Apple Cobbler

Preparation Time: 20 minutes

Cooking Time: 1 hour 30 minutes

Servings: 8

Ingredients:

- 8 Granny Smith apples
- One c. sugar
- Two eggs
- Two t. baking powder
- Two c. plain flour
- 1 ½ c. sugar

Directions:

Peel and quarter apples, place into a bowl. Add in the cinnamon and one c. sugar. Stir well to coat and let it set for one hour.

Add wood pellets to your smoker and follow your cooker's startup procedure. Preheat your smoker, with your lid closed, until it reaches 350.

Place apples into a Dutch oven. Add the crumble mixture on top and drizzle with melted butter.

Place on the grill and cook for 50 minutes.

Nutrition:

Calories: 152

Carbs: 26g

Fat: 5g

Protein: 1g

Pineapple Cake

Preparation Time: 20 minutes

Cooking Time: 1 hour

Servings: 8

Ingredients:

- One c. sugar
- One T. baking powder
- One c. buttermilk
- Two eggs
- ½ t. salt
- One jar maraschino cherry
- One stick butter, divided
- ¾ c. brown sugar
- One can pineapple slice
- 1 ½ c. flour

Directions:

Add wood pellets to your smoker and follow your cooker's startup procedure. Preheat your smoker, with your lid closed, until it reaches 350.

Take a medium-sized cast iron skillet and melt one half stick butter. Be sure to coat the entire skillet. Sprinkle brown sugar into a cast iron skillet.

Lay the sliced pineapple on top of the brown sugar. Place a cherry into the middle of each pineapple ring.

Mix together the salt, baking powder, flour, and sugar. Add in the eggs, one-half stick melted butter, and buttermilk. Whisk to combine.

Put the cake on the grill and cook for an hour.

Take off from the grill and let it set for ten minutes. Flip onto serving platter.

Nutrition:

Calories: 165

Carbs: 40g

Fat: 0g

Protein: 1g

Smoked Pumpkin Pie

Preparation Time: 10 minutes

Cooking Time: 50 minutes

Servings: 8

Ingredients:

- 1 tbsp cinnamon
- 1-1/2 tbsp pumpkin pie spice
- 15 oz can pumpkin
- 14 oz can sweetened condensed milk
- 2 beaten eggs
- 1 unbaked pie shell
- Topping: whipped cream

Directions:

Preheat your smoker to 325oF.

Place a baking sheet, rimmed, on the smoker upside down, or use a cake pan.

Combine all your ingredients in a bowl, large, except the pie shell, then pour the mixture into a pie crust.

Place the pie on the baking sheet and smoke for about 50-60 minutes until a knife comes out clean when inserted. Make sure the center is set.

Remove and cool for about 2 hours or refrigerate overnight.

Serve with a whipped cream dollop and enjoy it!

Nutrition:

Calories: 292

Total Fat: 11g

Saturated Fat: 5g

Total Carbs: 42g

Net Carbs: 40g

Protein: 7g

Sugars: 29g

Fiber: 5g

Sodium: 168mg

Wood Pellet Smoked Nut Mix

Preparation Time: 15 minutes

Cooking Time: 20 minutes

Servings: 8-12

Ingredients:

- 3 cups mixed nuts (pecans, peanuts, almonds, etc.)
- 1/2 tbsp brown sugar
- 1 tbsp thyme, dried
- 1/4 tbsp mustard powder
- 1 tbsp olive oil, extra-virgin

Directions:

Preheat your pellet grill to 250oF with the lid closed for about 15 minutes.

Combine all ingredients in a bowl, large, then transfer into a cookie sheet lined with parchment paper.

Place the cookie sheet on a grill and grill for about 20 minutes.

Remove the nuts from the grill and let cool.

Serve and enjoy.

Nutrition:

Calories: 249

Total Fat: 21.5g

Saturated Fat: 3.5g

Total Carbs: 12.3g

Net Carbs: 10.1g

Protein: 5.7g

Sugars: 5.6g

Fiber: 2.1g

Sodium: 111mg

Grilled Peaches and Cream

Preparation Time: 15 minutes

Cooking Time: 8 minutes

Servings: 8

Ingredients:

- 4 halved and pitted peaches
- 1 tbsp vegetable oil
- 2 tbsp clover honey
- 1 cup cream cheese, soft with honey and nuts

Directions:

Preheat your pellet grill to medium-high heat.

Coat the peaches lightly with oil and place on the grill pit side down.

Grill for about 5 minutes until nice grill marks on the surfaces.

Turn over the peaches then drizzle with honey.

Spread and cream cheese dollop where the pit was and grill for additional 2-3 minutes until the filling becomes warm.

Serve immediately.

Nutrition:

Calories: 139

Total Fat: 10.2g

Saturated Fat: 5g

Total Carbs: 11.6g

Net Carbs: 11.6g

Protein: 1.1g

Sugars: 12g

Fiber: 0g

Sodium: 135mg

Berry Cobbler on a Pellet Grill

Preparation Time: 15 minutes

Cooking Time: 35 minutes

Servings: 8

Ingredients:

For fruit filling

- 3 cups frozen mixed berries
- 1 lemon juice
- 1 cup brown sugar
- 1 tbsp vanilla extract
- 1 tbsp lemon zest, finely grated
- A pinch of salt

For cobbler topping

- 1-1/2 cups all-purpose flour
- 1-1/2 tbsp baking powder
- 3 tbsp sugar, granulated
- 1/2 tbsp salt
- 8 tbsp cold butter
- 1/2 cup sour cream
- 2 tbsp raw sugar

Directions:

Set your pellet grill on "smoke" for about 4-5 minutes with the lid open until fire establishes, and your grill starts smoking.

Preheat your grill to 350 oF for about 10-15 minutes with the grill lid closed.

Meanwhile, combine frozen mixed berries, Lemon juice, brown sugar, vanilla, lemon zest, and a pinch of salt. Transfer into a skillet and let the fruit sit and thaw.

Mix flour, baking powder, sugar, and salt in a bowl, medium. Cut cold butter into peas sizes using a pastry blender then add to the mixture. Stir to mix everything together.

Stir in sour cream until dough starts coming together.

Pinch small pieces of dough and place over the fruit until fully covered. Splash the top with raw sugar.

Now place the skillet directly on the grill grate, close the lid and cook for about 35 minutes until juices bubble, and a golden-brown dough topping.

Remove the skillet from the pellet grill and cool for several minutes.

Scoop and serve warm.

Nutrition:

Calories: 371

Total Fat: 13g

Saturated Fat: 8g

Total Carbs: 60g

Net Carbs: 58g

Protein: 3g

Sugars: 39g

Fiber: 2g

Sodium: 269mg

Pellet Grill Apple Crisp

Preparation Time: 20 minutes

Cooking Time: 1 hour

Servings: 15

Ingredients:

Apples

- 10 large apples
- 1/2 cup flour
- 1 cup sugar, dark brown
- 1/2 tbsp cinnamon
- 1/2 cup butter slices

Crisp

- 3 cups oatmeal, old-fashioned
- 1-1/2 cups softened butter, salted
- 1-1/2 tbsp cinnamon
- 2 cups brown sugar

Directions:

Preheat your grill to 350 oF.

Wash, peel, core, and dice the apples into cubes, medium-size

Mix flour, dark brown sugar, and cinnamon, then toss with your apple cubes.

Spray a baking pan, 10x13", with cooking spray then place apples inside. Top with butter slices.

Mix all crisp ingredients in a medium bowl until well combined. Place the mixture over the apples.

Place on the grill and cook for about 1-hour checking after every 15-20 minutes to ensure cooking is even. Do not place it on the hottest grill part.

Remove and let sit for about 20-25 minutes

It's very warm.

Nutrition:

Calories: 528

Total Fat: 26g

Total Carbs: 75g

Net Carbs: 70g

Protein: 4g

Rubs and Sauces

Smoked Tomato Cream Sauce

Preparation Time: 15 minutes

Cooking Time: 1 hour 20 minutes

Servings: 1

Ingredient:

- 1 lbs. beefsteak tomatoes, fresh and quartered
- 1-1/2 tbsp. olive oil
- Black pepper, freshly ground
- Salt, kosher
- 1/2 cup yellow onions, chopped
- 1 tbsp. tomato paste
- 2 tbsp. minced garlic
- Pinch cayenne
- 1/2 cup chicken stock
- 1/2 cup heavy cream

Directions:

Prepare your smoker using directions from the manufacturer. Toss tomatoes and 1 tbsp. oil in a bowl, mixing, then season with pepper and salt. Smoke the tomatoes placed on a smoker rack for about 30 minutes. Remove and set aside reserving tomato juices. Heat 1/2 tbsp. oil in a saucepan over high-medium heat.

Add onion and cook for about 3-4 minutes. Add tomato paste and garlic then cook for an additional 1 minute. Add smoked tomatoes, cayenne, tomato juices, pepper, and salt then cook for about 3-4 minutes. Stir often.

Add chicken stock and boil for about 25-30 minutes under a gentle simmer. Stir often. Place the mixture in a blender and puree until smooth. Now squeeze the mixture through a sieve, fine-mesh, to discard solids and release the juices, Transfer the sauce in a saucepan, small, and add the cream.

Simmer for close to 6 minutes over low-medium heat until thickened slightly. Season with pepper and salt. Serve warm with risotto cakes.

Nutrition:

Calories 50

Fat 5g

Carbs 2g.

Protein 0g,

Smoked Mushroom Sauce

Preparation Time: 30 minutes

Cooking Time: 1 hour

Servings: 4

Ingredients:

- 1-quart chef mix mushrooms
- 2 tbsp. canola oil
- 1/4 cup julienned shallots
- 2 tbsp. chopped garlic
- Salt and pepper to taste
- 1/4 cup alfasi cabernet sauvignon
- 1 cup beef stock
- 2 tbsp. margarine

Directions:

Crumple four foil sheets into balls. Puncture multiple places in the foil pan then place mushrooms in the foil pan. Smoke in a pellet grill for about 30 minutes. Remove and cool.

Heat canola oil in a pan, sauté, add shallots and sauté until translucent. Add mushrooms and cook until supple and rendered down. Add garlic and season with pepper and salt. Cook until fragrant.

Add beef stock and wine then cook for about 6-8 minutes over low heat. Adjust seasoning. Add margarine and stir until sauce is thickened and a nice sheen. Serve and enjoy!

Nutrition:

Calories 300

Fat 30g

Carbs 10g

Protein 4g

Smoked Cranberry Sauce

Preparation Time: 10 minutes

Cooking Time: 1 hour

Servings: 2

Ingredients:

- 12 oz. bag cranberries
- 2 chunks ginger, quartered
- 1 cup apple cider
- 1 tbsp. honey whiskey
- 5.5 oz. fruit juice
- 1/8 tbsp. ground cloves
- 1/8 tbsp. cinnamon
- 1/2 orange zest
- 1/2 orange
- 1 tbsp. maple syrup
- 1 apple, diced and peeled
- 1/2 cup sugar
- 1/2 brown sugar

Directions:

Preheat your pellet grill to 375 F.

Place cranberries in a pan then add all other ingredients. Place the pan on the grill and cook for about 1 hour until cooked through.

Remove ginger pieces and squeeze juices from the orange into the sauce. Serve and enjoy!

Nutrition:

Calories 48

Fat 0.1g,

Carbs 12.3g

Protein 0.4g

Montreal Steak Rub

Preparation Time: 5 minutes

Cooking Time: 5 minutes

Servings: 1

Ingredients:

- 2 tbsp. salt
- 2 tbsp. cracked black pepper
- 2 tbsp. paprika
- 1 tbsp. red pepper flakes
- 1 tbsp. coriander
- 1 tbsp. dill
- 1 tbsp. garlic powder
- 1 tbsp. onion powder

Directions:

Simply place all ingredients into an airtight jar, stir well to combine then close.

Use within six months.

Nutrition:

Calories: 19

Fat: 0.5g

Carbs: 3g

Protein: 1g

Conclusion

So now that we have reached the end of the book, I am very optimistic that you are well acquainted with some of the finest smoker grill recipes which will make you a pro at grilling, BBQ, and cooking in general.

Sometimes seeing so many recipes briefly can be very overwhelming. Therefore we had segmented this book into different sections each spanning recipes of a similar kind. So, go through the book as and when needed and make sure to follow the instructions in the recipe thoroughly.

I've put in a lot of love, effort, and time in this book to make sure that every recipe is as good as I wanted it to be. Of course, like always, most recipes allow you to do a little makeshift if suppose you are missing out on some ingredients. However, to get the best results, we want you to stick to the details as closely as it is possible for you.

So, make the most of this amazing cookbook and try these recipes so that you could take your food buds for a real ride.

I hope you enjoy cooking these recipes as much as I enjoyed jotting it down for you. I am telling this from personal experience that once you get hooked to the BBQ style of cooking; there is no way you're going to stay away from it.

Last but not the least, you have to make sure that you end up buying the best kind of smokers and use the perfect pellets or else you will lose out on getting the real authentic flavor for these perfect recipes. Tweak them a little if you so desire, but I believe they are as perfect as you would want them to be.